NATURAL WONDERS OF AMERICA

RUPERT MATTHEWS

Designed by
PHILIP CLUCAS MSIAD

Produced by
TED SMART and DAVID GIBBON

Exeter Books

NEW YORK

© 1984 illustrations and text by Colour Library Books Ltd.
CLB 1043
First published in the U.S.A. 1984
by Exeter Books
Distributed by Bookthrift
Exeter is a trademark of Simon & Schuster, Inc.
Bookthrift is a registered trademark of Simon & Schuster, Inc.
New York, New York.
Printed by Jisa-Rieusset, bound by Eurobinder-Barcelona-Spain
ISBN 0 671 07154 8

INTRODUCTION

The first settlers to arrive on the East Coast of the North American continent in the seventeenth century came for a variety of reasons. Some arrived looking for gold, others came in search of rich farming land and still others in search of freedom, but none of them came expecting to find the fantastic land that lay before them. The eastern seaboard has one of the most magnificent coastlines in the world, while the hinterland seemed rich in everything but gold. Even that was waiting to be discovered in almost unimaginable quantity far to the west.

The continent that spread out to the west of the earliest towns and villages would have baffled the first arrivals by its sheer size, if nothing else. The idea that such a huge and diverse land could be welded together into a single nation was probably beyond their comprehension. If they could have seen the stupendous natural wonders which lay across the land the early Americans would have been even more daunted.

North America is an ancient continent which has been worked upon by nature over millions of years to create a land of immense natural beauty. Long before the first signs of life appeared on earth, rugged rocks – which today form the Appalachians – were solidifying deep beneath the earth's surface. In time the rocks were uplifted, cracked, faulted, worn down and uplifted again to create the eastern band of mountains. Those to the west are younger in every sense of the word. The rocks that make up the peaks and valleys were formed millions of years after those of the Appalachians. The titanic earth movements that thrust the peaks up from the ocean floor began much later than those which created the eastern mountains; the Rockies were fairly level ground in the days of the dinosaurs. Both sets of mountains contain magnificent scenery which cannot be matched anywhere else on earth. Majestic peaks, encrusted with ice and snow, tower above glittering lakes and dark forests. Sheer cliffs rise from valley floors and are topped by craggy formations. In parts of the uplifts, rivers have cut great canyons from the living rock. In Arizona is the Grand Canyon, the largest in the world, whose beauty is numbing in its grandeur. The Colorado cut the fantastic feature from rising rock, and continues to cut to this day.

Between the two ranges of mountains stretch the central lowlands. This largely flat area of land is underlain by a block of immensely old rock, the core of the continent. The central lowlands have been flooded several times by vast inland seas. Deep bands of sedimentary rocks have been laid down and form the basis for the sweeping plains. Lined on east and west by mountains, the land of America contains some of the most fantastic natural wonders in the world.

In the Yellowstone country, geothermal activity has created a wonderland of spouting geysers and boiling mud. The country was first reported by the intrepid Jim Bridger, but Jim told so many tall stories that nobody believed the Yellowstone could possibly exist until a photographer visited the area. The activity of geysers and hot springs are among the gentler manifestations of a tremendous force that waits beneath the earth's crust. In 1980 Mount Saint Helens exploded with tremendous force, revealing the true nature of volcanic activity. The newest State in the Union has more than its share of volcanoes, but the Hawaiian volcanoes do not explode. Instead they gush forth a continuous stream of molten lava.

Far removed from the burning heat of the volcanoes are the many gentle waterways of the nation. The Florida Everglades support a unique flora and fauna which is unmatched by any other area in the world. The bayous of Louisiana have been built up by sediment from the greatest river in the United States: the Mississippi. Of all the great rivers of the world, the Mississippi is the most majestic and stately.

Sweeping across the center of the continent are the mighty prairies. Once the home of millions of buffalo, the prairies are now farmed by modern methods. They have become the grain basket, not only of America, but of the world. The fertile stretches of grassland suffer great extremes of weather. In the summer the merciless sun beats down upon the land, bringing scorching temperatures to the region. Six months later, the same land may well be blanketed by snow and frozen by temperatures as cold as the summer was hot. The United States has a great range of climatic conditions. New England is temperate, but destructive hurricanes of immense power lash the coasts around the Gulf of Mexico. In the Sierra Nevada winter can bring immense falls of snow, sometimes tens of feet in depth.

It is as a land of extremes that America makes its contribution to the natural wonders of the world. The world's largest trees grow in the mountains, while in the east the most beautiful fall in the world bedecks Vermont. Massively powerful volcanoes devastate miles of countryside, while mighty rivers bring life-giving waters to other areas.

The sheer grandeur of the mountains, the lakes and all the other wonders to be found within the United States is, perhaps, the country's greatest treasure.

CANYONS

When Captain Garcia López do Cárdenas wiped the sweat from his eyes and gazed at the awesome beauty before him, he probably cursed it viciously. Since the spring of 1540, he had been trekking northward across the burning deserts in search of the Golden Cities. The local Indians said that gold and silver lay just to the north, but blocking his path was a canyon so deep and wide that he could not hope to cross it. After three days of trying to find a path down the precipitous cliffs, Cárdenas turned round in disgust and went home.

Cárdenas never did find his Golden Cities, but he had found one of the greatest works of nature in the world. His impenetrable barrier was the Grand Canyon. The spectacle that filled Cárdenas with helplessness cannot fail to impress upon the modern visitor a similar feeling of insignificance. The beauty of the Canyon is truly stunning and unforgettable. Yet the despondent reports of Cárdenas brought no sightseers to the area. It was to be more than two hundred years before a white man gazed upon the Grand Canyon once again.

In 1776, Father Garcés came north in search of souls to be saved, only to find that they did not wish to be saved. In his wanderings he too came across the Colorado flowing between walls of rock. He described the sight as "the most profound canyons that ever onward continue".

These two Spaniards lived two centuries apart, a long enough period by human standards but a mere instant in the time scale of the Grand Canyon. It was more than ten million years ago that the Colorado began to cut the rock. At that time the river had no canyon but flowed quietly westward across level ground. Then the land around the river began to rise. Massive forces within the earth caused the rocks of northern Arizona and southern Utah to rise up into a massive bulge that can still be seen today. As the land rose, the river became steeper and more violent. Before long, geologically speaking, the Colorado was the raging torrent that it is today and the canyon building process could begin in earnest.

A fast-flowing river is one of the most destructive forces known to nature, and the Colorado is no exception. Every grain of sand carried in the water acts like a piece of sandpaper, rasping away at the riverbed and cutting into the banks. Every pebble that tumbles along behaves like a demented hammer, pounding against the bedrock with a force powerful enough to strip away the surface. Every fresh stone dislodged races downstream, blundering into others and displacing them. This violent process has been smashing away at the rocks of the Grand Canyon for millions of years.

The Colorado is no mere stream. Every day around half a million tons of sand and rock are hurled through the Grand Canyon, stripping away even more of the bedrock. In times of flood the amount of destructive rock coursing down the canyon is almost unbelievable. On one day in 1927 some fifty million tons of sand and pebbles tumbled down the Colorado. This is the equivalent of some hundred truck loads of debris each second. It is little wonder that the Colorado has been able to carve a path for itself that is nearly 220 miles long and a mile deep.

The canyon as a whole defies the imagination. It is just too big to comprehend. The tortuous course of the river writhes like a snake between vertical walls of rock. At Toroweap the cliffs fall sheer for three thousand feet. The river is so far below the rim that it appears to be a mere ribbon. The great ridges of rock that rise from the canyon writhe across the landscape, casting shadows and glowing with unearthly colors.

Throughout the long desert day the canyon changes as the sun crosses the sky. At dawn the cold sun throws long shadows across the depths of the canyon, masking the rushing river in blackness. Mid-day finds the strong sun beating relentlessly down on the landscape. The whole panorama is revealed, every crack and hillock stands clear against the heat. But it is at sunset that the canyon is at its most magical and beautiful. The fiery rays of the sun bathe the red rocks of the canyon in a rosy glow. Then, as the sun dips below the western horizon the canyon slips back into darkness.

For most, it is enough to stand on the rim of this mighty canyon and stare at the towering walls beneath. But hardier souls can travel into the depths. Mules descend the twisted paths that fall from the rim on day or overnight trips. One route crosses from rim to rim, cutting some two hundred miles off the road route.

But by far the most exciting way to see the canyon is to travel the river itself. Rafts take visitors on trips that may last three days or three weeks. The wild waters of the Colorado and the towering cliffs overhead are spectacular, but dangerous scenery.

Though the Grand Canyon of Arizona is the greatest of all American canyons, it does not have a monopoly of dramatic and beautiful scenery. Until just thirty years ago the Colorado, upstream from the Grand Canyon, wound through a canyon that was smaller but no less beautiful. Today, the Glen Canyon Dam has created a long, winding lake with sheer sides. Beyond this man-made wonder lie the untouched splendors of Canyonlands.

Spread over hundreds of square miles of southern Utah, Canyonlands National Park contains some of the finest canyons in the country. Perhaps the most stunning view is gained from Dead Horse Point. Here the Colorado has carved itself a great loop out of the layered limestones. The sweeping hairpin of the river encloses a sheer knife-edge of rock that reflects an ancient meander in the course of the river before it began to cut away at the rock.

The walls of Millard Canyon are a succession of towering, buttressed cliffs, but it is in Salt Canyon that the intricate natural sculptures are found. The beautiful arches and figures that abound in the area are not the products of brute force. The rushing waters and pounding pebbles that carved the Grand Canyon had little effect on Salt Canyon. Falling rain dissolves small amounts of carbon dioxide from the atmosphere. This produces a very weak solution known as carbonic acid. Limestone dissolves easily in acid, even in such a weak chemical as rainwater. Over the eons the falling rain has found the weak points in the rock and eaten them away. Once a gap is opened up, wind-blown sand and dust explores the hole and enlarges it. Rainwater collects and eats away even more of the rock. Before long undermined chunks fall away, leaving arches and weird shapes behind. Even the temperature of the desert takes a hand in the carving of the rock. The daytime heat causes it to expand, until the night comes and the rock contracts in the bitter cold. The alternate expansion and contraction of the stones creates cracks and splits, further eroding the canyon walls.

Salt Canyon is a maze of winding gullies and narrow dividing walls of rock. Wind eroded fissures line the walls which rise sheer from the canyon floor. Unlike the Grand Canyon, which may be approached by a number of ways, the only route into Salt Canyon, and its offshoots, is to drive up the bed of Salt Creek. The gaunt, bare walls of the canyon are dramatic enough, but the crowning glory of the area is to be found high up in the canyon. Angel Arch is an immense figure carved from the living rock. Beside the towering arch itself there appears to be the figure of a winged angel, its head bowed in prayer.

The stunning canyons of the area have been cut by streams and rivers which once flowed across flat lands. When a river flows across shallow slopes it forms many meanders and curves. These paths have been preserved in the routes of the canyons as they wind through the rocks. But the rushing waters can tear holes in the rock and shorten the course of the rivers. At Anderson Bottom Rincon, the Green River long ago broke through a rock wall, leaving its original course a dry canyon, well above the present canyon bed.

Dramatic as the canyons of the Colorado and its tributaries are, they lack the delicate intricacy of a canyon to the northwest which, strictly speaking, is not a canyon at all. Bryce Canyon is named after the hardy Scottish pioneer who came to Utah as a Mormon convert and tried for five years to eke a living from the inhospitable land. Ebenezer Bryce's only comment on the beautiful valley within his land was to describe it as "A hell of a place to lose a cow". The canyon has been described many times since Ebenezer Bryce moved on to Arizona, but seldom with the practicality of its first owner.

Millions of years ago the area around Bryce Canyon was covered by several large lakes. On the beds of these lakes silt collected and hardened, forming enormously thick bands of rock. The minerals and composition of the sediments determined the color and structure of the resultant rock. After millions of years the beds of silt and mud were so thick that the lakes ceased to exist. Only the broad, horizontal bands of sedimentary rock remained. Then giant earth movements cracked the newly formed rock and forced it up in a series of great plateaus. The rocks of the Paunsaugunt Plateau were slowly forced up into the sky and it is these that form Bryce Canyon.

Unlike the land to the south, the Paunsaugunt had no great river flowing across it. There could be no Grand Canyon here. Instead a multitude of small streams ate into the rock. The tremendous strains involved in uplifting the plateau created deep, vertical cracks in the rock. These cracks were eroded and expanded by the rivulets that fell from the plateau. Before long running water had torn into the rock and created great slits. But at Bryce there are many kinds of rock. Some are harder than others and resist erosion far better. The odd bulges and overhangs of the pillars are the result of softer rock being eroded from beneath harder, higher ones.

It is not only the weird formations that mark Bryce out from the other canyons. It has a delicate coloring that is unique. When the ancient rivers carried silt down to the lakes millions of years ago, they brought minerals with them. It is these minerals that color the rocks. Iron creates a variety of shades from fiery red, through gleaming yellows to dull browns. The purples are the products of manganese and the greens of copper.

Though the Grand Canyon, Canyonlands and Bryce Canyon all owe their existence, in one way or another, to the action of water, they also depend on a lack of water. The region of northern Arizona and southern Utah is one of desert and low rainfall. If there was as heavy a rainfall as on the California coast, the results could well be disastrous.

The delicate balance of erosion and uplift at Bryce would disappear. The sheer walls of soft rock would vanish into a bowl of weathered sand. The Grand Canyon and Canyonlands depend on the fact that the land is uplifting faster than the rain and wind erode it. If the trend were reversed, the steep canyon walls would disappear and the rivers would flow through broad, shallow valleys. It is the lack of water over millions of years that has created the spectacular canyons.

If the canyons of Arizona and Utah are deep, wide, winding affairs, the same is certainly not true of Texas. The Rio Grande rises in the San Juan mountains of Colorado and then swings south for the Gulf of Mexico, and even the mesas of southern Texas are no deterrent. Above San Vicente the river bores through the Mesa de Anguila in a narrow, sheer-sided canyon. If the towering walls are impressive from the river, and many boats make the perilous trip each year, the approach to the canyon from above is truly stunning. The undulating, scrub-covered landscape that seems to stretch on to the horizon suddenly stops. The ground simply drops away into a dizzying abyss that is many times deeper than it is wide. The gash in the earth's surface that is Santa Elena Canyon reaches depths of 1,500 feet.

Though Texas always seems to have the biggest and best of everything, even Texans must acknowledge the grandeur of Colorado's Royal Gorge. Dropping for more than a thousand feet from the surrounding countryside, the forbidding chasm has been carved by the Arkansas River as it courses through the Pikes Peak region of the state. A visitor center makes Royal Gorge one of the most easily reached of all the canyons in America. Spanning the yawning depths is the world's highest suspension bridge, from which the torrent below appears distant and remote. Descending the canyon walls is the world's steepest incline railway. At Royal Gorge it is easy to see a wonder of nature from above and below with little physical trouble.

But the tamed spectacle of Royal Gorge may not be able to capture the true atmosphere of the wild river canyons. This atmosphere is held in abundance by the Black Canyon of the Gunnison.

Like the Grand Canyon, the Black Canyon of the Gunnison has been cut from rising land by a powerfully flowing river. Indeed, the waters of the Gunnison flow into the Colorado and help to erode the Grand Canyon further down their course. It also shares the fate of the Grand Canyon in that its waters are dammed upstream of the canyon. In effect this has slowed down the rate of erosion so that the canyon is no longer growing as fast as it did. But the rocks through which the Gunnison cuts are quite different from those of the Grand Canyon. Hundreds of thousands of years ago the Gunnison cut a broad canyon through sedimentary rocks similar to those of the Grand Canyon. But as the land continued to rise the river cut deeper into the underlying rock until it struck strata of almost unbelievable age. The river had reached the solid, Pre-Cambrian core of the continent. The resistant, granite-like rocks of the core were totally different from the softer, sedimentary rocks above. The river no longer cut a broad canyon but forced its way down into the rock in a narrow gorge. The solid rocks of the Pre-Cambrian era were strong enough to form sheer drops without crumbling or fracturing. It is because of the rocks that the Black Canyon has such deep and steeply sloping walls. It is also the rocks that gave it its ominous name. Their color is a dark, brooding gray that seems to swallow the light. Moreover, the narrowness of the chasm forbids the entry of sunlight to the depths. In comparison with the sunny land above, the canyon is truly black.

The two-million-year-old canyon runs for some 53 miles through western Colorado, but is at its most spectacular for just 12 miles. This area has been included in the Black Canyon of the Gunnison National Monument. In this section the canyon reaches a depth of some 2,700 feet, though it can be as little as 40 feet across at its base. The managers of the canyon, which has been a national monument for more than fifty years, have made a point of preserving the wildness of the region. The roads that wind along both rims are kept at a respectable distance from the edge of the canyon and only rough, unimproved footpaths wind through the rest of the canyon.

A feature of such canyons is that they slice down through rocks created millions of years ago. This provides geologists with a marvellous opportunity to study the rocks that underlie a region. They are, therefore, able to piece together the ancient history of the region far more accurately. Not only that, but palaeontologists find many fossils in canyons as the rock in which they are trapped is removed by the water.

The Black Canyon is carved into rocks far too old to contain fossils; the dark granites were laid down before life began on Earth. But to the north, rocks a mere 150 million years old lie exposed and reveal the times of the dinosaurs. During the Jurassic period a strong river flowed through the region. The river was slow and several sandbanks interrupted its course. One of these sandbanks trapped the bodies of many of the animals floating downstream. More sand covered them and the bones slowly became fossilized. For millions of years, thousands of dinosaur bones lay undisturbed beneath the rock. The earth movements that created the Grand Canyon also gave rise to canyons in northern Utah and Colorado. In 1909 Earl Douglass was passing through the country when he noticed the fossilized bones of a creature caught in a canyon wall.

Over the following years scientists removed some 350 tons of dinosaur bones from the canyon. They revealed a complete picture of the area's fauna during the Jurassic period and included such beasts as Stegosaurus, Allosaurus and Brachiosaurus. Brachiosaurus may be the largest land animal ever, weighing over 80 tons and walking on pillar-like legs. The site is now part of Dinosaur National Monument. A section of the ancient sandbank has been left just as it was found, allowing visitors to see dinosaur fossils in their natural state.

Though the canyons of the Colorado Plateau region are among the most dramatic in the country, they are not the only canyons. Far to the northwest of the desert region is a land of forests and snows. Amid the towering bulks of the sequoias is a river known to the Spaniards as *El Rio de los Santa Reyes*, the River of the Holy Kings. Today it is called the Kings River and lies at the heart of Kings Canyon National Park in California.

Unlike the canyons of the southwest, which formed when the land around existing rivers rose, Kings Canyon is the result of a powerful mountain river carving a path through the slopes. The Kings River rises high in the Sierra Nevada and tumbles down to mingle with the waters of the Pacific far to the west.

Within the park the river flows in two courses, the South Fork and the Middle Fork. Both reaches have magnificent canyons. The South Fork is the most accessible and receives most visitors but it is the Middle Fork that has the wildest landscape and most majestic canyon. The canyons in the park can reach a depth of 8,000 feet as the waters gush down from the mountains. But the wild, narrow canyons do not reach right up into the mountains as they once did. Thousands of years ago the continent was in the grip of the Ice Ages. Massive glaciers formed in the high mountains and pushed their way down into the valleys. Where the rivers of ice once rolled, the narrow gorges have been broadened out into wide, U-shaped valleys where high meadows and forests flourish. The change from narrow canyon to broad valleys is sudden and marks the furthest point reached by the glaciers.

Of all the canyons in the mountains of the northwest, perhaps the greatest and best-known is the canyon of the Columbia River in Washington and Oregon. The Columbia River rises far to the north, in British Columbia, and covers some 1,200 miles on its journey to the ocean. It is the only river that has managed to cut a path through the mighty Cascade Range and its canyon is of immense importance as a communications route. The canyon itself is famous for its numerous waterfalls. Along the route of the river many small streams come down to meet it. Where they reach the edge of the canyon they fall in feathery showers over the edge of the precipice.

All along its route the river is lined by roads and railroads as they take the easiest route through the mountains. The path through the mountains was traveled by Lewis and Clark on their famous expedition. Setting out from St. Louis, they crossed the continent to find out just exactly what was there. The reports they brought back were largely responsible for the flood of settlers that traveled the Oregon Trail at the end of the last century. But the intrepid Lewis and Clark were not the first men to cross the western mountains. The Scottish Canadian, Alexander MacKenzie, had earlier determined to find a Pacific outlet for his profitable fur trade. Unfortunately, the first river he followed was the mighty northern river that bears his name today. He crossed hundreds of miles of wilderness only to find that the river flowed into the Arctic Ocean and was no good for his trading interests. It was on his second attempt that the Scot discovered a route through the Western Cordillera.

Like many other rivers in the region the Columbia has been dammed for hydroelectric purposes. Indeed, Washington and Oregon produce a large percentage of America's water generated electricity.

The eastern states are not as barren or untamed as the western areas, and they cannot boast the range and variety of canyons that are found in the west. But it is in the east that one of the most awe-inspiring of American canyons is to be found. The gorge carved by the mighty Niagara River forms the border between the United States and its northern neighbor. In times past it formed a natural, fortified border across which no army could march, but today it is more a symbol of co-operation than of strife.

The vast power of the river as it courses between Lake Erie and Lake Ontario is almost beyond comprehension. The river flows down a steep gradient along most of its path, the only exception being just below the great falls, where the water is calm enough for pleasure boats. Below this Maid of the Mist Pool, as it is known, the river courses through the Niagara Gorge for some five miles, dropping 93 feet in the process. It is hardly surprising that the steep gorge walls and turbulent waters have been such a barrier. The Niagara is the only outlet for the waters of Lakes Erie, Huron, Michigan and Superior. In turn, the Great Lakes drain over a quarter of a million square miles of North America. All the rain and snow that falls on this vast area must pass through the Niagara to reach the sea, so there is plenty of water to push back the falls and enlarge the gorge. The drop of the river between the two lakes, over 300 feet, is used for hydroelectric purposes, but this does not detract from the beauty of the gorge.

This gorge is different from those of the west in that the river has not carved it through direct erosion of carried sand and rock. The waters of the Niagara simply do not have the grit and pebbles that make the Colorado appear so muddy, and make it so destructive. The Niagara has gouged out its gorge because of the falls. The mighty cascade that roars over the lip of the Niagara Falls is wearing away at the base rock, as it has been doing for millenia. As the water eats away at the rock the falls are retreating slowly upstream. In the path where the falls have been there is now the gorge, marking the route the falls have taken since they began to retreat from the edge of the Niagara Escarpment at Lewiston.

Part of the way along its route the river makes a right angle turn to the northeast. At this spot the waters swirl and eddy with frightening speed and power to form a huge whirlpool which bars the river to any kind of traffic. Atop the steep canyon walls, wreathed in vegetation, it is difficult to see why the river should make such a diversion. In fact the reason dates back to a time before the Niagara even existed. The river came into being at the end of the last Ice Age. Before that time the waters of the Great Lakes region drained into the Mississippi, but the retreating glaciers opened up the northern route and the river began to flow. Before the glaciers had advanced a powerful river ran northeastward across the path of the Niagara. Where the new river meets the old channel it suddenly shifts direction and it is this that causes the whirlpool.

The complex geology and drainage patterns of America have created a wealth of gorges and canyons that is perhaps unique. The dramatic splendors of the Grand Canyon can be equalled by no other canyon on earth, while the delicate carvings of Bryce Canyon and Canyonlands are amongst the most beautiful formed by nature. Even in the east, the powerful Niagara has carved a gorge for itself. The canyons of America are an essential and valued part of her natural heritage.

VOLCANOES

At half past eight on a sunny spring morning a complete side of the mountain was ripped away by a titanic explosion. Thousands of tons of rock were blown into the sky as the pent up pressure was released in a devastating second. The shock wave reached out across the land like a hurricane. Trees were wrenched out of the ground and flung aside like matchsticks, and all the time the sky grew darker. For more than thirty miles the terrifying wind spread destruction, toppling trees and flattening buildings. Two hundred miles away early risers turned their heads in wonder as the noise of the explosion rumbled across their city. Then came the mud. Millions of tons of boiling, liquid mud coursed through the valleys, sweeping away everything in its path. The burning hot gas, bringing the suffocating ash with it, outstripped many an automobile and killed its passengers.

By the time it was all over 150 square miles of forest had been flattened as if a giant hand had squashed it, and thousands of square miles were covered in soft, choking ash. The mountain had blown over a thousand feet off its height and one and a half cubic miles of rock had been scattered to the four winds.

The eruption of Mount St. Helens on May 18, 1980 was one of the most powerful in history. The blast was 500 times more powerful than the bomb which wiped Hiroshima from the face of the earth. For days a column of ash and smoke belched out of the crater that was thousands of feet tall and hundreds of feet wide. The cataclysmic eruption not only devastated much of Washington State, it also affected the weather of the entire world.

The violence of volcanoes is perhaps the most dramatic and awesome manifestation of the power that nature holds over America. In a matter of seconds such a force can be unleashed that man is helpless to do anything but flee. Yet the mechanism of volcanoes is well understood and, to an extent, eruptions can be predicted, though not controlled.

Magma, or liquid rock, welling up from deep beneath the earth's surface is the cause of all volcanic activity, but it comes in a variety of forms. Mount St. Helens was long known to be a volcano. Indeed, the whole Cascade Range is volcanic in origin. But it had been dormant for as long as anyone could remember. It was this fact which was to create the conditions for the 1980 explosion. At Mount St. Helens a huge, subterranean magma chamber had been slowly emptying itself through a vent, or shaft, in the earth's surface. The emerging molten rock had spread out and solidified, building up the 9,677 foot peak. Then, for some reason, the vent became clogged. Rock solidified in the magma's escape route and trapped it deep within the earth. As time passed pressure began to build up. In many other parts of the world, at Hekla in Iceland for example, the plugs are weak affairs and give way easily. At Mount St. Helens the plug in the vent was immensely strong. Pressure was able to build up against it with a force that is unimaginable. When the plug eventually gave way it released forces powerful enough to hurl rock and ash 63,000 feet into the air.

But Mount St. Helens had given warning that she was about to erupt. Months before the great explosion, scientists began to pick up small earth tremors on their seisomographic machines. Little notice was taken of them. In an area as geologically unstable as the West Coast small quakes occur nearly every day. As time passed the number of earth tremors centered around the mountain increased and scientists became interested. On March 20, and for several following days, the whole mountain shivered. With hindsight it is clear that the plug was coming under immense strain, but at the time nobody knew quite what the tremors meant.

On March 27 the first signs of an eruption were noted. By March 30 a small column of smoke and ash was rising from the top of the mountain. As the ash continued to rise through to mid-April, tourists and newsmen flocked to the area. At the same time the earth tremors became more frequent. Geologists began to fit events into a pattern and they speculated that lava might soon begin to flow.

By the end of April it was clear that something was going to happen. Earthquakes measuring over 3 on the Richter scale were being measured at a rate of 40 every day. More ominously, a bulge had appeared on the north face of the mountain. The bulge grew larger and larger, and hotter and hotter until, on May 7, it was 400 feet tall. By now the Governor of Washington had closed the entire area within ten miles of the peak, but some residents refused to move. The next day another small eruption began, throwing rock and ash high into the air. Perhaps the volcano was letting the pressure out slowly, perhaps there would be no big eruption. On May 17 residents were allowed back into the prohibited area for the day. The morning of May 18 appeared no different from any other in the previous week or more. Steam and ash continued to pour out, the bulge was no larger and there was none of the expected lava. The great explosion came without warning, catching many literally sleeping.

When the destructive explosions had finally stopped, the top of the mountain had ceased to exist. Instead, there was just a yawning chasm, open to the north. But the volcano was still active and nobody really knows what the future holds for the shattered mountain.

Mount St. Helens is deservedly the most famous of the Northwestern volcanoes, but it is not the only one. Mount Hood, whose peak hangs over Portland, Oregon, had a small eruption just sixty years ago. This peak is still the source of several hot springs which emphasize its volcanic nature. About the same time that Mount Hood was letting off steam, Mount Lassen experienced a succession of minor eruptions.

Despite the destructive power of the Mount St. Helens blast, it would be wrong to think of volcanoes as purely negative forces. The soil that results from eruptions is extremely rich. In a few years the devastated lands around Spirit Lake will be bursting with fresh and luxuriant growth. The scars of May 18, 1980 will soon heal because of the nature of the very ash which destroyed so much. Indeed, one of the most beautiful sights in Oregon was a devastated wilderness like Mount St. Helens a few thousand years ago. Around 4,000 B.C. Mount Mazama blew up with an explosion comparable to that of Mount St. Helens. The top of that mountain was blasted away, leaving a similar yawning crater. Today, that crater has become Crater Lake, one of the great tourist attractions of the region.

Just sixty years ago another of the northwestern peaks suddenly erupted, though without the force of Mount St. Helens. It was May 30, 1914 when Mount Lassen began to show signs of life. In the first year of activity more than a hundred eruptions took place. These were mainly small affairs, throwing out steam and ash. Almost a year later, on May 19, 1915, lava welled to the surface and flowed to the northeast and southwest. To the southwest the lava flowed for some thousand feet before it cooled and solidified, but to the northeast is was a different story. The lava melted vast amounts of snow and ice. The resultant mudslide swept down the mountainside and destroyed everything in its path. Three days later the volcano suffered a great explosion of pent up steam and ash which hurled debris some 30,000 feet into the air. For another two years Mount Lassen boiled away until it finally settled down. Today, the dramatic evidence of the eruption is included in the Lassen Volcanic National Park.

Other National Parks with volcanic origins can be found hundreds of miles to the west on the Hawaiian Islands. Unlike Mount St. Helens or Mount Lassen, however, the Hawaiian volcanoes have been erupting for millions of years, though they have not always been in the same place.

The whole surface of the Earth is made up of several "plates". These plates, on which stand all the continents and oceans of the world, are slowly shifting. Where two plates rub against each other, as in California, earthquakes can result. In other areas, such as the northern boundaries of India, mountain chains can be thrown up. One of the largest of these tectonic plates is the Pacific Plate. This is moving, at a speed of about three inches a year, to the northwest.

Underlying the plates of the earth's crust, at a depth of many miles beneath the surface, is the mantle. This is a mass of hot, molten rock upon which the tectonic plates literally float. At a great depth, far beneath the floor of the Pacific is a "hot spot" in the mantle. Nobody is quite sure what this hot spot comprises? Whatever it is, it is extremely powerful, turbulent and unstable. For millions of years it has been pushing upward against the earth's crust, punching holes through the miles of rock and spurting magma onto the ocean floor. As the thousands of millions of tons of molten rock poured out of the ocean floor it solidified and formed mountains. The Hawaiian Islands are simply the peaks of vast submarine volcanoes which rival Everest in size.

Over the years the awesomely powerful hot spot has stayed in exactly the same place, but the Pacific plate has moved over it. This means that an outlet which was once right over the hot spot gradually moved away to the northwest and the turbulent, molten rock had to punch a new hole in the earth's crust. The oldest island that was caused by the hot spot is far to the northwest of Hawaii: Midway. This tiny island is merely the weathered stump of a much larger land. Over millions of years, the waves pounded away until it was eroded to its present size.

The hot spot, meanwhile, was busy building fresh undersea mountains to the southeast. About a million years ago, it began work on what is now Haleakala. For thousands of years the molten rock welled up and solidified, each fresh eruption making the mountain that bit larger. But when the mountain top reached the surface the combination of heat and seawater produced tremendous steam explosions which racked the Pacific. For hundreds of years more the eruptions continued, until Haleakala grew so large that it joined with the older volcano of Pu'u Kukui to form the island of Maui.

At one time Maui covered more than 2,000 square miles and included the present-day islands of Lanai, Molokai and Kahoolawe. Today, however, Haleakala is suffering erosion as the main vent for the hot spot has again shifted, to Hawaii Island itself. But Haleakala is still active in a small way, a major lava flow breaking the surface as recently as 1790. Furthermore, the mountain shows off many features typical of volcanic areas.

Across the barren slopes are numerous lava flows, still in their bare state because not enough time has passed to turn the rock into rich, volcanic soil. Beneath the solidified level of the lava are several hollow, cylindrical tubes. These form when the top level of lava solidifies, leaving a narrow flow beneath the surface. The still liquid interior runs away, leaving the upper crust suspended over the tube. In places the roof gives way and the lava tube can be entered. Near Holua Cabin a 400 yard long tube is large enough to walk through. In other places the noxious gases in the lava form massive bubbles within the flow. The skin of these bubbles can solidify and leave a cave beneath. Several such caves can be seen at Haleakala. Right across the barren hill are found scattered boulders and rocks. These are the lava bombs that are thrown out whenever the volcano erupts. Lumps of molten lava are flung high into the air and solidify before smashing to the ground again. Other bombs do not have a chance to cool and splash out into an irregular circle of stone when they land; these are known by the descriptive, if unflattering, name of "cow-dung bombs".

Where plants can gain a foothold on the stone of the volcano, one of the first is the rare silversword. Found only on the slopes of Hawaiian volcanoes, this beautiful plant grows as a low, spherical plant until, after several years, a tall flower spike grows upward from the bush. This spike bears a multitude of magnificent golden flowers before it falls and the plant dies.

Not far from Haleakala is the traditional home of Pele, the ferocious fire goddess of Hawaii. It is at Kilauea and Mauna Loa that the tempestuous forces of the hot spot reach the surface. It is these volcanoes, sending spectacular sheets of liquid rock into the air and pouring lava down the mountain slopes, that feature most often in the news bulletins of the world. In just five years the side vent of Mauna Ulu grew 400 feet in height and covered 10,000 acres with molten rock. Kilauea stands some 22,000 feet above the ocean surface and is still growing. But the Pacific Plate continues to move, and the hot spot is already building fresh undersea mountains to the southeast of the smouldering Hawaii. In a few thousand years Mauna Loa and Kilauea will be silent and new islands will have risen above the rolling ocean.

Magma, welling up from deep within the earth, does not always produce such powerful and destructive phenomena as the volcanoes of the Northwest or Hawaii. The now dormant Mount Lassen no longer spouts lava, but hot water gushes from the ground in abundance. The minerals deep within the volcanic rocks are dissolved in the boiling liquid. As the steaming waters flow down the slopes they lose the minerals. Many a waterfall and stream bed in Lassen Volcanic National Park is stained red with iron oxide; perhaps the best example of this is East Sulphur Creek, whose waterfall glitters pink in the sunlight. Other stream beds may be stained blue, yellow or even black, depending on the mineral dissolved in their waters.

Far away in the Zigzag Mountains of Arkansas a million gallons of hot water gush to the surface every day at a constant temperature of 143° Fahrenheit. Hot Springs has tamed its heated waters and has become a spa town. The water here, unusual in that it does not smell or taste obnoxious, comes from deep within the ground. Heated by magma at a great depth, this water flows to the surface through a natural fault in the rock, rather than having the close contact with magma that the waters at Mount Lassen can boast.

The commercially viable springs in Arkansas cannot touch for sheer power and spectacle the spouting waters of Wyoming. Yellowstone National Park is best known for its 10,000 geysers, sulphur springs, fumaroles and pots of boiling mud. The great Yellowstone basin is the remains of a volcano that exploded, in a similar manner to Mount St. Helens, some 600,000 years ago. The remnants of the volcanic activity that dealt such a hammer blow to the area are the geysers and hot springs of the basin.

It is thought that the magma that fed the volcano is today just three or four miles beneath the ground. The reservoir of magma is thought to be cooling down. When magma solidifies, the water and gases that form a major part separate out. Tremendous pressure builds up and the burning hot gases and liquids are forced up to the surface through cracks in the rocks. At Yellowstone the rising gases meet large amounts of rainwater which is stored in the rocks; the result is the dramatic geysers of the region.

Nobody is quite sure why some boiling springs suddenly erupt in mighty geysers. Most of the theories advanced, such as a tall column of water suddenly heated at its base, could only apply to a few geysers. Scientists are generally agreed, however, that the action has something to do with underground caves that absorb the pressures of steam build up and the bubbling of dissolved gases; in other words a similar effect to that achieved by opening a bottle of soda water.

However they are caused, geysers are among nature's most spectacular works. The most famous of all geysers within the national park is, of course, Old Faithful. This powerful geyser erupts at intervals of between 45 and 80 minutes and will play for some five minutes. The great, steady column of boiling water may reach 150 feet in height and is one of the greatest sights in the park. Not far away Grand Geyser will send up a far more spectacular display. The fountain reaches at least 200 feet into the air and is broader than Old Faithful. Unfortunately as much as 12 hours may pass between eruptions, and it is impossible to state when the next is due. It does not, therefore, have the attraction of Old Faithful as a tourist feature.

Like the waters at Lassen Volcanic National Park, the geyser water often brings up minerals and calcium which it deposits around itself. At the 90 foot tall Castle Geyser this material has built up around the vent to form a hollow tower which gave the geyser its name. Grotto Geyser, on the other hand, has deposited its material on the trunks of surrounding trees, and this has created a fairytale surrounding to the geyser, with arches and pillars, that is truly fantastic.

It is not only geysers that the area owes to its hot water. Many of the quieter springs have a beauty that the spectacular geysers cannot hope to match. The broad-mouthed spring known as the Morning Glory Pool is one of the beautiful natural sights of the world. The crystal clear water comes to the surface in a pool shaped like an inverted cone. The water is suffused with a beautiful blue that no artist has yet matched; it has to be seen to be believed. But it is unfortunate that visitors seem intent on destroying such a marvel. Objects are thrown into the pool and sink to the bottom. They block the influx of hot water and allow the pool to cool to such an extent that algae is gaining a foothold and turning the blue pool a muddy green. On the other hand, algae is critical to the beauty of the Emerald Pool in the Black Sand Basin. At this pool the algae produce a magnificent, rich green color that glows all the brighter when a blue sky reflects the true glory of the green. Another attraction is Punch Bowl Spring. At this boiling vent the geyserite material has been deposited around the margins of the pool, where the water cools. Over the years this ring of material has grown and accumulated until the pool is trapped within a vertical wall of rock.

At Mammoth Hot Springs the building properties of hot water are to be seen even more clearly. About 500 gallons of water come to the surface here every minute. The water originally falls as rain and snow on the slopes of Terrace Mountain. From here the water seeps into the underlying band of limestone that stretches under the mountain. Here it comes under the influence of the magma and begins to heat up. As the temperature rises it dissolves carbon dioxide gas from the magmas and calcium from the rock. When the water emerges along faults in the rock it begins to cool and the dissolved chemicals are deposited as calcium carbonate. The stone that forms from this material molds itself into a series of giant steps up the hillside. Looking like a magnificent staircase, the rock is naturally pure white, but at Mammoth Hot Springs it is colored with a rich tapestry of brilliant reds, yellows and blues. The fantastic coloration is due to algae that thrive in the hot water. Where the water has changed its course the terraces are a dull, crumbling gray.

From the violent explosions of Mount St. Helens and the lava flows of Hawaii to the hot springs of Arkansas and Wyoming, the volcanic actions of America have had a profound effect on the landscape and constitute the most magnificent natural spectacles in the country.

RIVERS

In any country the most important natural resource is undoubtedly its rivers. The system of running water is far more crucial to the development of the country than any deposits of minerals, however valuable. Without water there could be no plant life and, therefore, no agriculture of any kind. Furthermore, all human settlements need water, not only for drinking, but for washing and cooking. In the United States an average town will consume about 200 gallons a day for each inhabitant, so the water requirements of even a medium-sized town are phenomenal. No matter how rich mineral deposits may be, it is impossible for a large town to grow up in the middle of a desert, unless water can be obtained from somewhere.

In the United States, more than perhaps any other country on Earth, the role and influence of rivers has been of outstanding importance. The first settlers came in search not only of freedom and liberty, but also of good farming land. Of necessity farms require water and so the settlers marked out their settlements along the banks of the rivers. It wasn't long before the first Americans began to feel confined along the coastal strips around Jamestown and Plymouth. To the west were vast reaches of rich land waiting to be cleared and plowed, so that men could make a proper living. In the earliest days there were no good roads into the interior and nobody had thought of inventing the railroad. The only way to transport people and equipment was to load them onto boats and sail along the rivers. Rivers became the highways of America and for many years formed the basis of exploration. Paddling their birchbark canoes, the earliest explorers crept westward into the great unknown.

Frenchmen came down from Quebec and explored the Mississippi Basin, while Spaniards came up the river from the Gulf of Mexico and their fabulously rich empire. It was not until after the Louisiana Purchase of 1804 that Americans could really push westward to fulfil their manifest destiny and populate the great lands beyond the Mississippi. First, however, the region had to be explored.

When Lewis and Clark left St. Louis they took the only available route into the wilderness: the Missouri. Like earlier explorers of the continent, Lewis and Clark loaded their equipment, weapons and supplies into boats and sailed off into areas no white man had seen before. They traveled up the Missouri as far as the Dakotas, meeting and attempting to make friends with the Indians they encountered. Unfortunately the Sioux, then as always, proved particularly warlike and had to be threatened with a cannon before the expedition could move on toward the Continental Divide. They had to abandon their boats at the mountains, but once across the ranges they built new boats and traveled down the Clearwater River to the Snake and on to the Columbia, finally reaching the Pacific on November 15. They returned by way of the Yellowstone and Missouri Rivers, to reach St. Louis more than two years after they left.

If the rivers are the backbone of the United States economy, growth and settlement, the Mississippi is surely the backbone of the rivers. The largest river on the North American continent, the Mississippi and its tributaries drain some one and a quarter million square miles of 31 states and two Canadian provinces. This makes it fifth in the world, as far as drainage area is concerned, and with three hundred and fifty thousand million gallons of water pouring into the Gulf of Mexico every day it is eighth largest in terms of water. In its many forms and faces the Father of Waters exhibits many facets of river formation. It is not only the largest river in America, it is one of the most fascinating.

The headwaters of the Mississippi proper flow across a landscape that thousands of years ago was devastated by the crushing weight of ice. During the Ice Ages the whole northern section of the Great Plains was covered by immensely thick glaciers. Beneath the glaciers the rock was scraped and ground to dust and the debris dumped at the southern end of the ice sheet. When the vast quantities of ice melted some ten thousand years ago, massive rivers were suddenly formed. These waterways carried away the great amounts of water that were released from the melting glaciers and bored through the moraine of debris. The channels formed by those ancient rivers are followed by the Upper Mississippi, as well as by the Wisconsin and Illinois Rivers.

In the west the tributaries of the Mississippi rise among the soaring pinnacles of the Rockies. Crystal clear mountain streams gush, sparkling down the steep slopes to combine amid the foothills and flow out across the plains. It is these western tributaries that are, perhaps, the most important to the Mississippi as a whole.

Surprisingly, however, the rainfall is rather low in the areas they drain; often as little as 25 inches a year. The fact that three-quarters of this falls during the summer months means that the western rivers fluctuate with the season, and so does the Mississippi itself. The waters that flow from the Appalachians come together to form the Ohio before entering the Father of Waters. This means that, although more water enters the Mississippi from the west, the Ohio is the greatest tributary. It pours a quarter of a million cubic feet of water every second into the main river, compared with the Missouri's seventy thousand.

From its source to St. Paul, Minnesota, the Mississippi is a clear river which bears little resemblance to the Ol' Man River of popular imagination. Flowing in a winding course through low-lying scenery and past swamps and lakes, the river is unnavigable and quiet. From Minnesota southward to St. Louis the river gradually increases in size and power. The clear waters are still to be found as the river flows through limestone bluffs, but the Missouri changes the character of the river completely. For hundreds of miles the Missouri flows across the plains, wearing away at the soft soil and rock over which it passes. By the time it reaches the Mississippi, the Missouri is loaded with tons of silt and sand. Below St. Louis, the Father of Waters becomes the muddy torrent that it remains all the way to the Gulf of Mexico.

In its lower courses the river becomes the archetypal "old river". Its great flow, often a mile and a half wide, rolls majestically across a landscape that is almost totally flat. The river loops and meanders across the plain in the most tortuous manner imaginable. In places it abandons its original course and snakes off into another loop. The abandoned section becomes a long, thin lake which eventually silts up until it is simply a marshy hollow. The river often floods here and deposits silt wherever the floodwaters reach. Along its lower course, therefore, it develops naturally raised banks, or levees, which hold back the waters until the next flood, when the river may change course yet again. The ability of the river to build land is more dramatically shown far to the south in Louisiana. As the river slows near its mouth it drops vast quantities of mud and silt, perhaps as much as five hundred million tons a year. Over the years this deposited soil has accumulated and built up until it has constructed hundreds of square miles of marsh and swamp out of what was once the open sea.

For centuries it has been recognized that the Father of Waters is of great importance to the North American continent, but the first white man to set eyes on the majestic river did not even live to regret it. In May 1541, Hernando de Soto was leading a Spanish expedition north from Mexico in search of the fabled Seven Cities of Cibolla. It was said that the treasure of the Seven Cities was even greater than that of the Aztecs. In his hunt for the gold de Soto reached the Mississippi near what is now Memphis, Tennessee. Instead of finding the Cities of Cibolla, de Soto only found his death. His body was slipped into the waters of the great river by his companions, who retreated down the Mississippi under a hail of Indian arrows.

More than a hundred years later Louis Jolliet came down from French Canada and reached the mouth of the St. Francis River before turning back. Less than a decade later the famous adventurer René Robert, Sieur de la Salle, canoed down the entire river to the delta and at once claimed the whole region for the King of France. The French presence is today remembered in the names of several towns, such as St. Louis and the state name of Louisiana. It wasn't until after the Louisiana Purchase that the United States began to take a large part in the story of the Mississippi.

In 1811, the first steamboat to ply the river waters appeared on the Mississippi. As if to signal the opening of a new era, the ship's maiden voyage was accompanied by a fearsome earthquake which changed the course of the Father of Waters. Though the first steamship on the river, *New Orleans* was not alone for long. Within ten years nearly 200 steamships visited the city of New Orleans and in 1832 well over a thousand shiploads of goods came to New Orleans from the interior. That same year the source of the Great River was finally found by one Henry Schoolcraft. Working as an Indian Agent, Schoolcraft found that the mighty torrent began in a small lake near the Canadian border. In keeping with his name, Schoolcraft used Latin when naming the lake. He called it Lake Itasca, from the Latin for "true head": *verITAS CAput.*

The sternwheelers made transport downriver amazingly cheap and the whole wealth of America west of the Appalachians poured down to New Orleans. Riverside towns boomed in wealth and prosperity and even the devastation of the Civil War and the following Reconstruction could not hamper the river trade. In 1870 the competitive side of the steamers reached its dramatic height in the race of the *Natchez* and the *Robert E. Lee.* The *Robert E. Lee* won the three-day race by stripping down and burning her wooden superstructure.

Even as the majestic sternwheelers coursed up the river with smokestacks belching fire, their day was passing. The center of population and wealth was shifting west and railroads were taking the trade from the river. By the end of the century it seemed as if the end of the river trade was in sight. But the First World War brought fresh life to the river, a prosperity that has not diminished with the years. By 1931 more cargo was being shifted along the river than at the height of the paddlewheeler era. In the process something has been lost. The elegance that attended the passage of the twin-stacked steamers was lost with the advent of the small diesel tugs that have taken their place.

Today, the working boats can push rafts of barges that measure three hundred by fifty feet and hold as much as two thousand five hundred tons of goods. The supervision of the river traffic has been in the hands of the Mississippi River Commission since 1879. This authority keeps a channel three hundred feet wide and twelve feet deep open as far as Cairo, and a nine-foot-deep channel as far as Minneapolis. The commercial future of the river seems assured; waterways through the Ohio and Illinois Rivers link the Father of Waters to the Great Lakes and the St. Lawrence Seaway and the volume of goods transported along the river continues to increase.

The system of canals and locks which connects the Great Lakes with the sea is known as the St. Lawrence Seaway, having augmented the St. Lawrence River which handled early waterborne trade. The mighty Seaway constitutes one of the greatest engineering feats in American history. Since 1783 the Canadians had been embarking on a series of projects which made it easier to get goods from the Gulf of St. Lawrence to the Great Lakes. These took the form of small canals and locks bypassing rapids and falls. It wasn't until the United States joined in the construction work in 1954 that the St. Lawrence Seaway really got underway. By the close of the decade, a colossal $446 million had been spent and the Great Lakes were open to ocean shipping. Instead of off-loading their cargoes at East Coast ports, ships could take their goods direct to Midwest destinations.

Between Lake Superior and the Atlantic Ocean the waters drop by over 600 feet. To overcome this, massive locks were built. The great locks can take ships up to 730 feet long and 75 feet broad, while the channels dredged through the river itself can accommodate ships with a draft of 25 feet. The section of river through the Thousand Islands area has been opened up by removing whole sandbanks and shoals that would otherwise forbid the passage of large ships.

The whole project was undertaken for a variety of reasons. Uppermost, there was the desire to provide cheap export transport for Midwest grain. Indeed some fourteen million tons of grain was soon finding its way out through the Seaway. Even more iron ore from Labrador and Quebec is shipped the other way to find a market in the United States. Not far behind in terms of bulk moved is coal, with over eleven million tons passing through the region each year. The construction of the system has had an enormous impact on the Midwest, far more than the natural St. Lawrence River ever did.

Perhaps the most dramatic part of the Seaway is the Welland Canal which bypasses the greatest wonder on any of America's rivers; the Niagara Falls. The first words ever written about this marvel of nature describe it as "a vast and prodigious cadence of waters", a description still fitting today. The mighty torrent that throws itself over the precipice forms the only outlet for the whole drainage basin of the Great Lakes, an area of some quarter of a million square miles. As much as 250,000 cubic feet of water may be flowing down the Niagara River every second in the summer. Coming from the Great Lakes, as it does, the water has had no time to pick up any sediment and the river is crystal clear. The sheer whiteness of the falls has been a major factor in their popularity.

The Niagara Falls are by no means the tallest in the world, but the sheer spectacle of so much water crashing over such a wide curtain is unsurpassed. The American Falls measure a thousand feet from bank to bank and stand a hundred and sixty-seven feet tall. A recent rockfall scattered the base of the falls with a jumble of boulders and rocks. On these jagged edges the tumbling waters bounce and play, sending a great shower of spray high into the air. In the sunlight the spray creates a permanent rainbow arching its way across the falls, and in winter spray can freeze and the falls become enveloped in a mantle of ice and snow. The same fallen rocks have made impossible the feat of plunging over the falls in a barrel. In days gone by the barrel would have fallen into a deep pool of water; today it would be smashed on the jagged rocks. On the other side of Goat Island lies the dramatic sweep of the Horse Shoe Falls. These are slightly shorter, at 162 feet, but have a bank to bank measurement of 2,600 feet.

The falls first formed when the glaciers retreated. Until that time the waters that drained from the Great Lakes area flowed south along the Mississippi, but with a route to the north opened up the Lakes drained in that direction. Where the river met the edge of the escarpment it fell in a spectacular fall. Erosion may well have turned those falls into steep rapids, but the Niagara has always been undercutting the wall of the waterfalls and the vertical drop has been maintained.

Apart from its scenic grandeur the Niagara is of economic importance as well. Above the falls giant tunnels and canals divert water from the river and transport it to powerful hydroelectric generating stations. The various authorities sensibly decided to leave about 100,000 cubic feet a second flowing in daylight during the tourist season and 50,000 otherwise. In this way the beauty of the unique falls was preserved while the needs of man were satisfied. It is estimated that an average of 130,000 cubic feet of water are diverted every second for the use of the power stations. Their great complexes can produce up to four million kilowatts and supply the needs of local industry. In fact, several electrochemical works have opened specifically to make use of the hydroelectric energy coming from the river.

Far to the west, on the other side of the continent, another of the great rivers of America has been tamed and harnessed to produce hydroelectric power. The Columbia River is the largest river to flow into the Pacific from North America and is one of the continent's chief sources of hydroelectric power. In its 800 mile length within the United States it is capable of generating a third of all hydroelectric power produced in the country. It is one of the most highly-developed rivers; only 80 feet of its 1,290 foot descent is not used for hydroelectric purposes.

Grand Coulee Dam is the largest of the eleven dams that "step" the river to make it easier to manipulate. It stores water for use in the winter when the river flow is at its lowest. The expensive construction projects along the Columbia pump their power, through high-voltage federal transmission lines, to the cities of California. Useful as all this development is, it has its drawbacks. One of the most controversial is the effect of the systems on the fish. All early explorers to the region were amazed by the numbers and quality of the salmon to be found in the river. In 1866, when most of the Northwest was unexplored wilderness, a salmon cannery was operating on the Columbia. Within twenty years thirty canneries were exporting 43 million pounds of salmon to the kitchens of the world. The dams are denying the fish their original spawning grounds and the population is dropping alarmingly. Fortunately, schemes are underway to provide "salmon routes" around the dams. Quite how much this will help remains in doubt, but the salmon should soon be returning to the Columbia.

Rising in the snow-encrusted mountains of Colorado is a clear, babbling brook which tumbles down the mountain slopes just like any other. This particular stream, however, is destined to become one of the great rivers of America. The Rio Grande flows for nearly two thousand miles across the states of the Southwest and forms the entire border of Texas and Mexico. As with so many of the natural wonders of the Southwest, the Rio Grande was first seen by a Spaniard. But Alvar Nuñez Cabeza de Vaca was not traveling in search of any fabled treasure. De Vaca had been quietly attending to his own business when he found himself shipwrecked on the shores of the Gulf of Mexico. In his wanderings through the unknown lands of Texas, he came across the Rio Grande quite by accident.

In its journey from the San Juan Mountains to the sea, the river crosses some truly spectacular country. After passing through the San Luis Valley in Colorado, the Rio Grande cuts two canyons, the Rio Grande Gorge and White Rock Canyon, before flowing out onto open land again. This stretch of its course is across burning desert and rocky wastes. After gouging through another sequence of canyons known as Big Bend the river reaches the coastal plains across which it meanders to the gulf.

Like so many other rivers in America the Rio Grande is dammed, but not for hydroelectric power. The water from the dams of the Rio Grande is used to irrigate the surrounding, parched land. A series of treaties with Mexico has made possible the production of crops as diverse as potatoes, cotton and citrus fruits in otherwise barren land.

From the very earliest times the rivers of America have been of critical importance. The prehistoric Indians used them for agriculture and without them the bounties of nature could not have been enjoyed by the hunting tribes. To the whites they were important for irrigation, trade and exploration. Even today, these marvels of the natural world remain of vital importance to the American nation.

FORESTS

After stepping ashore on Plymouth Rock, one of the first things that the Pilgrim Fathers did was to chop down trees. The timber they yielded was of immense importance to the first settlers in America. They built their homes out of it, stockaded their livestock with it and relied on it for their tools. If it hadn't been for the great forests of New England, European settlement may never have got started at all.

The great natural commodity of woodland, with its cranberries and turkeys, seemed inexhaustible to the Pilgrim Fathers. The dense forest stretched from the shoreline back into the interior. For several generations Europeans lived along the East Coast and made a living among the trees without ever finding the western edge of the woodland which they were exploiting so profitably. Yet even in their wildest dreams, those early settlers cannot have imagined the great bulk of timber that lay to the west.

The eastern woodlands reached from the coast, over the Appalachians to the fringes of the Great Plains. Beyond the sweeping grasslands there were vast areas of forest among the mountains and foothills of the Rockies and the Pacific Coast. Timber was one of the most important natural assets given to the early settlers and the exploitation of the resource has never slackened. After three centuries of felling and clearing the area of land swept bare of trees is large, yet that still covered by forest is vast. Thousands of square miles have never heard the steady thud of the axe and trees grow in their natural way. The annual harvest of this timber is measured in millions of cubic yards, but this is barely one percent of the timber standing in the United States today. The trees are well able to look after themselves and yearly replace the trees that are felled by man.

Of all the timber that stands in the United States the grandest and most majestic is to be found in the far west. Thousands of miles from the trees that brought success to the Pilgrim Fathers stand the largest trees in the world: the Sequoia. It is only among the mist-shrouded mountains of the west that the giant sequoia has been able to survive. During the days of the dinosaurs it was spread throughout the world and sheltered many a Brontosaurus or Allosaurus. More highly-evolved trees have pushed it to extinction in other parts of the world, but it has survived on the slopes of the Sierra Nevada and brings a sense of mystery to any who visit its realm.

It is the vast size of the giant sequoias that marks them out from any other thing on earth. Indeed, the tree dubbed the General Sherman is the largest living thing known to man. It is 275 feet tall and measures 36 feet in diameter at its base. It has been estimated that this gives the tree around 50,000 cubic feet of timber in its trunk alone. The giants of the forest only grow in certain highly localized areas. It is thought that there are less than a hundred groves of these trees in the world. The fact that they do not grow anywhere else is due to the special needs of the giant sequoias. They require a long growing season between spring and fall to produce enough food to sustain their enormous bulks. Above the 7,500 foot elevation there are very few giants simply because the snows last too long for the tree to survive. Likewise, a prolonged cold snap with temperatures below zero will easily kill a magnificent redwood.

But perhaps the most critical time for a redwood is when it is a seedling. It is on the survival of the seedlings that the future of the redwoods really depends. The undergrowth of the Sierra forests is extremely dense and lush. Any sequoia seed falling among the riotous growth would have little hope of surviving. The struggle for sunlight and moisture would be easily won by other species. Luckily, the undergrowth of the forests is prone to catching fire, which it does every five or six years. The roaring flames not only clear the forest floor of the undergrowth, they also help the sequoias more directly. The tree holds onto its seeds after they have matured, unlike most plants which will disperse them as soon as possible. The heat of the fire causes the cones to dry out and spring open. The redwoods, therefore, automatically shed their seeds when there is the best chance of them surviving. Each redwood can shower over four million seeds after a fire, so they have every chance of taking root.

Once it has found a patch of bare earth and germinated, the trials of the young sequoia have only just begun. They are very slow-growing and at the end of their first year the roots are no more than a foot long. The slightest lack of moisture will kill a young sequoia. Even if it survives all the hazards of the elements, a hungry deer can ruin a seedling's chances in a few seconds of nibbling.

The scorching fire which is a bonus for the young seedlings is, of course, a danger to the mature trees. To combat the risk the sequoias have developed their famous bark. The cinnamon colored trees are clad in a spongy bark which is resistant to heat and flames. Even so, really ferocious fires can break through the barrier and leave ugly scars, such as on the General Grant tree.

Once past the hazardous first months of life the young sequoia becomes one of the fastest growing trees in the forest. It shoots up at an alarming rate of two feet a year until it reaches the height of the General Sherman. This seems to be the best height for a sequoia to be, for there it stops. For the rest of its life it grows outward, adding to its girth every year. The oldest examples are thought to be nearly three thousand years old and have been growing fatter for centuries.

It is this tendency to expand outward that has given the sequoias their popular appeal. People love to compare giants to things with which they are familiar. The fact that it is possible to drive an automobile through the base of one of these trees brings home just how big they are. In another part of the forest a fallen tree was taken over in 1858 by one Hale Tharp. He closed the end of the hollow trunk and installed a chimney. For several years the hardy explorer lived a comfortable existence in the tree.

Even Hale Tharp had to admit defeat when it stared him in the face in the shape of a Sierra winter. Not that it is all that cold up in the realm of the redwood. The problems start with the snows. By late November the first light storms presage what is to come and most sensible people quit the area at the earliest signs of snow. By the time spring comes around an average winter may have seen some twenty feet of snow lying on the ground. In 1969, Sequoia National Park received a staggering 38 feet of snow before the summer thaws brought life back to the forest. The firs and evergreens that crowd around the redwoods bow under the pressure. The sheer weight of snow bends down the branches of the conifers until they resemble a smooth pyramid in outline; the identity of the tree lost amid the snow. But the giant redwoods stand supreme. The bare trunks stand clear of snow, their cinnamon lines the only relief from the vistas of white. Congress has even gone so far as to designate the General Grant as the "Nation's Christmas Tree", it is such a beautiful sight in the snows.

Large and majestic as the redwoods are, they are only a tiny part of the vast tracts of forest that stretch across the mountains. They are not even the tallest trees in the forest. That honor goes to the near relative of the giant sequoia, the *Sequoia sempervirons*, or coast redwood. The slender, elegant trunk of the coastal relative may reach a towering 350 feet above the ground. Nor are they the oldest trees in the mountains. High above the range of the giants grow the bristlecones, which may be twice as old as the oldest redwood and, some claim, are the oldest living things on earth.

Reaching right across the northwest, up into Canada, is one of the largest stands of native timber in the entire world. The coniferous forests of the mountains are among the most effective plant communities in existence. A mixed conifer forest, as this is, makes the most of any sunlight that reaches it to produce food and fresh growth. About ninety percent of all sunlight is absorbed by the trees and undergrowth and utilized by the chlorophyll of the leaves. Only about five percent of solar energy is actually wasted, the remainder being used for transpiration and evaporation. This accounts for the prolific growth of the forests among the mountains. It is only where the soil is marshy or non-existent that the trees have failed to get a foothold.

The great natural asset that these trees presented was soon realized by the early settlers. Most of the cities of the Northwest began life as logging camps or ports for timber exportation. After all, the tall, straight conifers were ideal for making tall, straight masts and spars. The wooden ships of the world relied on the conifers for their main motive power until someone discovered that masts made of numerous small sections stood up to storms much better. Even so, the rich timber of Oregon remained a vital export for the area. Today, the legacy of the forest is not forgotten by the people of the Northwest and tree felling or log chopping contests are favorites at local shows and fetes. Deep within the forests of the Olympic Peninsula and the valleys of the hills the roar of the chainsaw signals the modern prosperity of the industry which began with the steady thudding of axe upon timber. Amid the tall, cool forests the stillness of the air lends itself to legend. It was through these woods that the greatest lumberjack of them all once strode, sweeping to left and to right with his mighty axe. Paul Bunyan was accompanied in his travels by his faithful blue ox, Babe, who followed patiently, always ready to help out in the logging business. It was said that Babe was so large that his eyes were six feet apart. Paul himself used young pine trees as combs and when he spoke his voice was so loud that twenty men fell over backwards. Many tales were told about this giant of a man as he roamed the forests and he has even been credited with creating the Black Hills out of an upside down mountain by having a fight on the top of it.

The forests of Paul Bunyan reach across the Continental Divide to the borders of the Great Plains, but in the passing of miles the character of the forest changes. It is no longer the cool, shady conifer forest of the Northwest. The slopes of Colorado are clothed in shivering aspens. Come the fall of the year the steep slopes of the eastern Rockies are a riot of gold as the leaves of the aspens prepare to fall. The particular yellow that blankets the hills is not mirrored in the evergreen forests to the west and has a beauty all its own.

The vast forests of the mountains in the west are a rich source of food for any herbivorous animal which cares to take advantage of the plants, and for any carnivorous animal which takes advantage of the well-fed herbivores. Of all the animals that frequent the forests, perhaps the rarest is the huge woods bison. This imposing animal is actually a subspecies of the rather more prolific plains bison. The majestic beast, together with its cousin, was once on the verge of extinction. Today, however, several small herds are cared for in various National Parks and the subspecies is staging something of a comeback. The shaggy bovine has to eat practically all day in order to maintain its great bulk. This is even more of a problem than for the plains bison as the woods bison is significantly larger. A really big bull may top the 3,000 pound mark.

If the woods bison is one of the most noticeable of the animals in the forest, there is one mammal which makes a living out of being unseen and is therefore not as rare as is generally thought. The cougar slinks around the mountains on its silent feet in search of the deer and other animals on which it feeds. In the past it was hunted by farmers and ranchers who, quite rightly, suspected it of taking their livestock. It is by nature a lonely animal and hunts mainly at night, quite unlike the timber wolf which may run in packs of up to 16 animals. As its name suggests, the timber wolf prefers the forests to anywhere else for it is easier to surprise and bring down game among the undergrowth than out in the open country of the plains. Though attacks by wolves on man are rare, they are by no means unknown and the lonesome howl of a timber wolf baying to the moon is one of the eeriest sounds in the United States. It brings to mind all the loneliness and savagery of the wild.

Neither the cougar nor the timber wolf, powerful as they may be, are the largest or the most powerful meat-eaters of the forests. The bear is undoubtedly the animal to be most feared if come across in the wild. Black bears, which may in fact be any color from black through brown to cinnamon, are perhaps the most common and feed mainly on plants. They are particularly fond of berries, but have been known to make a meal out of anything that looks edible. At about 6 feet in length, the black bear is a large enough animal to encounter in the forest, but such a length seems puny beside that of the grizzly. The nine-foot long and four-foot tall grizzly is the most powerful beast in America. The areas where it roams have been drastically cut back since the days of the early mountain men whose "bear stories" were as famous, entertaining and just about as true as *Snow White* or *Sleeping Beauty*.

The great beasts are only found in the densest and least-visited parts of the Northwest. Here they live a quiet life free from the encroachments of humans and pursue a lifestyle very similar to the black bear, although they are known to take rather more in the way of live meat than their smaller cousin. For many years it was thought that the danger of the grizzlies, and their sheer power, was something of a scare story. The fantastic qualities of the early explorers' stories certainly seemed more in the realms of fairy stories than real life. The great bear had been peacefully pushed from his habitats in the Dakotas and most other places in America; even the national parks authorities played down the threat of the grizzlies. Until one night in 1967, when two grizzlies killed and ate their human victims. Suddenly the grizzly was a real danger again. The rarest of American carnivores soon became even rarer as man realized the powers of nature and pushed the bear back again.

Far in the Northwest there may, or may not, be an inhabitant of the forest even rarer than the grizzly. The first stories of the sasquatch came back at the same time as the mountain men's tales of the feats of bears, and were given as much credence. The idea of grown men being besieged in a log cabin by giant apes was, after all, a little far-fetched. In recent years, however, the sasquatch or bigfoot has staged something of a comeback. Sightings have become more frequent and there has even been a movie shot of the wild apeman, the authenticity of which has been argued over ever since it was taken. The most common form of evidence for the existence of the sasquatch is still the hundreds of footprints that are found by streams and rivers throughout the area. Some of the footprints are eighteen inches long, making the apeman some ten feet tall. There can be little wonder that the beast, if it exists, has earned itself the name of "bigfoot."

Giant man-apes apart, the wildlife of the rugged Northwest and its forests is every bit equal to the grandeur of their mountain backdrop. The forests of the East were once rich in wildlife too. They echoed to the cries of great beasts and rustled as the wild creatures pushed between the dense undergrowth. But the settlers soon put a stop to that and it is only now that the original inhabitants of the area are managing to make a comeback. Tennessee was once so infested with bears that the ability of Davy Crockett to "grin down a b'ar" excited the admiration of many a backwoodsman who came face to face with one, armed with nothing more deadly than a single-shot musket. Just as Davy Crockett moved on because he felt hemmed in by all the people, so did the bear. But it was a much smaller animal that bore the brunt of the white man's attentions in the early years.

The beaver was not only a common animal among the streams and lakes of the Eastern forests, it was a great influence upon them. Before the coming of man, and the Indians are only recent arrivals, no other animal can have affected its environment to such a degree as the beaver. Not that the beaver knew what it was doing, as far as he was concerned he was just getting on with the business of life. In order to survive, the beaver found it necessary to fell trees almost as quickly as Paul Bunyan and to dam rivers with a zeal which only hydroelectricity has instilled in man. The ponds which they created ranged in size from little more than a puddle to lakes acres in extent. The rivers were slowed down and artificial habitats created for the fish. Unfortunately for the beaver, there was a fashion back in Europe for beaverskin hats. Civilization was paying good money for beaver pelts, so first the Indians and then the white men moved into the forests to hunt the furry animal. For years the trade prospered, but then the supply of beavers ran out. Their dams collapsed and the rivers ran free. Trappers had to move further west in search of pelts and the Eastern forests were bereft of their beavers.

Despite the hunting of the wildlife and the felling of trees by both settlers and modern inhabitants, the woods of the East have one great glory which is unmatched by any other forest land on earth. The pine trees of the West stay green throughout the year, but in Vermont the fall brings out a rainbow of colors. The forested slopes of the valleys are checkered with reds, golds and oranges as the leaves reach the end of their life cycle. Fall in Vermont is one of the most famous natural events in America. People will travel hundreds of miles just to be in that tiny state for a few magical weeks, but very few of the visitors actually understand what is going on in the leaves.

Broadleaved trees have to shed their leaves in the winter because the sharp frost would damage them beyond repair if they remained on the branches. The trees can then concentrate on producing new leaves for the spring. It would obviously be better if the trees did not let any goodness or minerals fall with the leaves. As the colder weather comes on the leaf undergoes a variety of changes. First, the green chlorophyll which converts sunlight into sugar is broken down and withdrawn from the leaf, and this allows the natural yellow of the leaf to show through. Next, sugar trapped in the leaf cells reacts with the sunlight and produces red tints. Finally, the tree pumps into the leaves any waste products that it wishes to remove; these are generally brown in color. The kaleidoscopic range of colors depends simply on how much of any one change is occuring in the leaf at the time. The results of such mundane chemical changes is a riot of color which takes the breath away.

The multitude of different forests that blanket such areas of the nation are among America's finest natural resources. They were vital to the early settlement of the country and have maintained their economic importance for centuries. Most of all, however, they are beautiful and the endless vistas they offer are the finest of their kind in the world.

WETLANDS

America is not generally reckoned to be among the marshy countries of the world. Holland has been reclaimed from miles of marshy salt flats and the country is still dependent upon dikes and ditches to keep the water back. Nor is it as waterlogged as the Amazonian country of Brazil. Nevertheless, America has such a wide diversity of geology and landscape that it is no wonder that it contains some of the loveliest and most typical marshes and swamps in the world.

In the past, such areas of nearly stagnant water have been regarded as less than useless and ambitious draining schemes have been embarked upon. The fact that malaria and other diseases are endemic in wetlands has been another factor in their draining. Now, however, Americans are beginning to realize the true worth of their natural heritage. Any great area of standing, or slow moving, water is useful because it increases the rate at which water is absorbed by the ground. Even the most desolate of bogs is productive enough to warrant the harvesting of peat. America gathers some half-million tons of peat each year. Though the energy gained from burning this product is tiny compared to that gained from oil or coal, it is still a factor in the preservation of wetlands.

Another important bonus for the wetlands of America is the fact that they support a unique and wonderful wildlife. Among the trees and grasses of the swamps roam rare and beautiful animals found nowhere else on earth. It is perhaps this more than anything else that has prompted the government to take action to preserve the great wetlands of the nation.

Across the northern reaches of the Great Plains lie dozens of marshy areas. Resembling stagnant pools more than anything else, these small marshes are a legacy of the Ice Ages. Thousands of years ago the advancing glaciers scoured the plains and scooped out hollows in the bedrock. It is these hollows that form the marshy areas. Over the past century or more the majority of these small swamps have been drained for agricultural purposes. It is in other parts of America that the great natural tracts of swamp and marsh are to be found.

The first marshes to be encountered by white men in North America were those along the coasts. On April 26, 1607 Captain John Smith of England landed near what is now Cape Henry in Virginia. He had arrived to see whether it was a suitable site for a settlement. Unfortunately, he had only just landed and begun to survey the area when "There came savages creeping upon all fours with their bows in their mouths." Deciding that discretion was the better part of valor, Captain Smith climbed aboard his ship and sailed off to found Jamestown.

The area where Captain John Smith landed and was attacked is now included in the Seashore State Park of Virginia. The same park includes one of the finest and most accessible areas of cypress swamp in the Eastern states. The swamp, which is served by a planked walkway, lies just behind the sandy deposits that have been thrown up by the sea along the coast.

Despite being so close to the sea the cypress swamps are freshwater and, in an emergency, the water is quite drinkable. The clear water lies to a depth of about three feet across the forest floor, but below it is a treacherous quagmire of mud and silt. Normally such a shifting surface could not possibly support anything as heavy as a tree, but the bald cypress is superbly adapted to life in the eerie swamp.

The base of the trunk flares out into a wide platform which shares the load of the tree's weight across as much area as possible, giving the trees a secure base on which to grow. Once the roots actually reach the mud they are faced with yet another problem; there is no oxygen in the water-sodden soil. Most tree roots gain their oxygen from pockets of air in the soil, but the bald cypress has to push its roots back up into the air. The roots appear as bald cones rising above the surface of the water. Such trees can live to be hundreds of years old. Eventually, a tree will become too large and heavy for the mud to support it and will topple over. But even then it does not necessarily die. If its roots can continue to draw water the tree may produce fresh shoots that grow upward to form "secondary trees" on the trunk of the old. Each year the cypress shed their leaves, which fall into the water and sink to the mud below. In time they decompose and add to the richness of the soil.

Festooned among the trees of such water forests is Spanish moss, which is not really a moss at all. This plant is not a parasite and does no damage at all to the tree on which it lives. The moss merely uses the tree as a convenient perch above the water. It derives moisture and nutrition by itself.

Not far from the Seashore State Park is the ominous sounding Great Dismal Swamp, so named by Colonel William Byrd who came here in 1728. Forty years later George Washington visited the swamp as part of a surveying expedition which was sent in to decide whether it would be feasible to drain the swamp for productive land. At that time the Great Dismal Swamp covered 2,000 square miles of Virginia and North Carolina, but by the end of the century nearly 40,000 acres had been drained.

Today, the swamp covers some 750 square miles of coastal plain in the two states. Its greatest features are, perhaps, the cypress, water ash and juniper trees standing above the water and marshy ground, cloaked in a tangle of honeysuckle. Among the trees and creepers live a variety of rare animals, and a frightening array of deadly snakes. Of more benefit to humans are the large numbers of tasty fish that swim in the waters of the 37-mile-long swamp. At the heart of the maze of waterways and channels that form the Great Dismal Swamp is Lake Drummond, which covers some 9 square miles.

Further south, in Georgia, near Homerville, is found the mighty Okefenokee Swamp. Unlike the Great Dismal Swamp, which lies near the end of a drainage system, the Okefenokee spreads across the head of such a system. In fact it is not so much one large swamp as a series of marshes and swamps that, together, form the source of the Suwannee River.

The swamp's name is an apt description of the area; it is derived from the Muskagean Indian name which means "watershaking". Large areas of the swamp's 600 square miles are covered by the shallow water and tall cypress trees to be found further north. Like the cypress trees in Virginia, these are also festooned with hanging Spanish moss. But the Okefenokee has a great range of plantlife. There are vast tracts of what appears to be grassland but is really wet and treacherous underfoot. In other places ridges of sand show above the water as small islands. Tucked away amid the trees, grasses and water is an immense variety of flowering plants, including some of the world's rarest and most beautiful orchids.

The swamp is formed in a shallow dip in the rock some 40 miles long and 25 miles wide. In this great natural water trap the conditions necessary for a swamp – slow moving water and a high water table – have become stabilized and it would take a massive effort on the part of man to make any sort of an impression at all.

But if the 600-square-mile Okefenokee is formed in a dip in the ground, quite the opposite is true of perhaps the greatest freshwater swamp in America.

Far to the south, at the southernmost tip of Florida, lie the great Everglades, covering some 4,000 square miles of the state. The underlying rock of the Everglades is a vast slab of limestone. This mass is nearly level, only sloping some two inches a mile to the south. Across the gigantic plate flow the waters of the Everglades. The Everglades are perhaps best thought of as a huge river flowing slowly from Lake Okeechobee to the sea. In its journey it spreads out across the great limestone slab to form a river a few inches deep but nearly 50 miles wide. As with most swamps, the underlying soil and muck is amazingly fertile and large areas of the beautiful region have been drained and agriculture now takes advantage of the rich soil. To counteract the drainage schemes, some million and a half acres of the primeval swamp and marsh have been set aside in the Everglades National Park.

The Everglades of Florida are a world to themselves. There is nowhere quite like them anywhere on earth. The flora, landscape and fauna of the Everglades are unique and well deserving of the National Park status that has been conferred upon them. As with all National Parks, emphasis is placed on the enjoyment of the natural landscape, while at the same time preserving its beauty for the future.

The range and variety of plants and animals in the Everglades is truly remarkable. There are not only the cypress swamps that are also found to the north but a whole range of habitats and ecosystems dependent on the slow flow of fresh water from the north.

Perhaps most typical of the Everglades are the vast stretches of saw grass. Wherever the fresh water is shallow enough this formidable plant will push down roots and grow to a height of 15 feet. The grass, strictly speaking a sedge, gained its name from the profusion of sharp serrations which line the edges of the leaves and make it particularly difficult to pass through. Weaving between the stands of grass are channels of water free from vegetation; these are the channels where the water is too deep for the sawgrass to gain a foothold. As in the Okefenokee, the monotonous panorama of water and sedge is broken by the outcrop of sandy bars. Known locally as "hammocks" these islands stand some three feet clear of the water and support many plants not found in the swamp proper, including numbers of palms, live oaks and mahogany. Some of the largest mahogany trees in America grow on these isolated islands. Other islands amid the swamp are caused by low-lying hills of the bare limestone bed. On these islands pine trees proliferate. From Turkey Point in the east to an area around Ficus Pond, an irregular band of pine trees marks the presence of a ridge of limestone. In many cases the towering pines seem to be growing out of the bare rock, but this is just an illusion. In fact the roots of the trees creep into crevices and cracks in the rock where soil has accumulated. While the vegetation on the sand islands can easily be destroyed by fire, that on the limestone thrives on it. An uncontrolled fire will destroy the undergrowth and allow the weaker pine seedlings to gain a foothold.

North of Big Lostmans Bay the waterlogged marshes of the Everglades are covered by the familiar cypress trees and Spanish moss that is to be found in many other regions.

To the south the fresh water spills out into Florida Bay to mingle with the salt waters of the Atlantic and Gulf of Mexico. To the west, however, the slow flow of the fresh water is slowed even more as it runs into the dense mangrove swamps of the Gulf coast. The mangroves are an important land-building plant and have been extensively grown as wave and storm breaks. A mangrove swamp is an impenetrable mass of vertical stems and thick, gooey mud. The many branched stems and roots of the mangroves (it is often difficult to tell the difference) catch any sediment brought down by the waters and hold it back from the ocean. As the thick mud builds up it loses its salinity and normal Everglades growth takes over. Meanwhile, the seaward edge of the swamp creeps gently out to sea, reclaiming more and more land.

But if the plant life of the Everglades is rich and varied, its animal life is truly astounding. When English settlers first came to Florida the Spaniards, who had been there much longer, told them that a large lizard or *el lagarto* lived in the swamps. The English misunderstood the Spanish and have referred to the great reptiles as alligators ever since. The alligator is possibly the most dangerous and ferocious animal in the Everglades. A large twelve footer has such powerful jaws that it would easily be able to bite the leg off a cow, if it ever got a chance. Most of the time, however, alligators in the Everglades are content with devouring fish and birds. Apart from taking prey, alligators are important to the ecology of the area. During the dry season they will dig out small hollows in the Everglades where water can collect. These "gator holes" are important as refuges for fishes and birds when the water level falls. Crocodiles can also be found in the Everglades, but they are very rare.

Though the alligator is the most dangerous inhabitant of the swamps, it is by no means the largest. The gentle, plant-eating manatee grows to a length of 17 feet. Unfortunately, the propellors of motorboats pose a great threat to this inoffensive creature.

It is as a refuge for rare and endangered species that the Everglades are perhaps at their best. The beautiful snowy egret is staging a comeback as is the roseate spoonbill. Though the odd flamingo is seen they are no longer regular visitors to Florida. The long-endangered Florida panther still haunts the deeper and less accessible areas of the Everglades.

It was in this natural fastness that the Seminoles were able to hold at bay the might of the American Army for years. Using the islands as market gardens and haunting the waters in their canoes, the Seminoles were the followers of the Calusa tribes. These earlier peoples had suffered terribly from white man's diseases and were all but extinct by the time the Seminole arrived in the early 1800s. By 1860 the forty year war with the Seminoles was effectively over, although no treaty was ever signed, and white immigration could begin. This immigration has had a profound effect on the Everglades, more because of man's need for fresh water than his need for land. The drained areas of swamp total barely a fifth of its original area, but the water drained off to quench the thirst of Miami is having a slow but definite effect on the vast Everglades.

If the effects of man's work on the Florida Everglades are uncertain and nebulous, they are even more so in the Louisiana swamps to the northwest. The swamps around the mouth of the Mississippi are very obviously the products of a river, far more so than the Everglades. The mighty Mississippi drains nearly a million and a quarter square miles of America, making it the fifth largest drainage area in the world. Much of this enormous area is land that is easily eroded. As a result, the river that pours half a million cubic feet of water a second carries vast amounts of sediment in it. Near the end of the long journey from the mountains and plains the waters of the Mississippi slow to around 3 miles per hour. At such a speed the water can no longer suspend the sediments and they begin to fall out.

Over the years the deposited sediment builds up on the seabed until it breaks the surface of the ocean and creates new land. The river now flows over this newly constructed swamp and deposits its load further on, creating even more land. It is this long, slow process that has built up most of southeastern Louisiana and is responsible for keeping it there.

Because of its very nature a slow-moving, winding river will often change its course. Whenever it does this it will begin to build up a new delta some distance from the old one. As the new delta expands, the ocean eats away at the old delta and gradually destroys it. This process has happened many times to the Mississippi delta. Nine thousand years ago the river flowed directly south from Baton Rouge and built up a delta that extended some forty miles beyond the present coastline of Vermillion Bay. Five thousand years ago the delta switched to the area north of New Orleans and created the peninsula that nearly cuts Lake Pontchartrain off from the sea. By the time of Christ the river had again changed course and built up a swampy landmass that reached out to the Chandeleur Islands. The weathered stump of this delta is the peninsula east of Lake Borgne. The present course of the Mississippi, southwest to Pilot Town, was established about a thousand years ago. Then, in the aftermath of the Civil War, the river again changed its course, or tried to.

The bulk of the sediment-carrying water began to flow down the Atchafalaya river. But the citizens of New Orleans depended on the clear shipping channel of the Mississippi for their livelihood. The river was dredged and water diverted back past New Orleans. Not only that, but anti-flood levees were built up. These two interferences with the river's natural course have resulted in the sediment being carried straight out to sea, beyond the continental shelf. This means that the vast swamps below New Orleans are being eroded as if the waters were cut off, without a new delta building up around the Atchafalaya.

Channels dug to allow shipping and pipe lines access to the city have allowed salt water to penetrate the lovely marshes and kill off many of the plants. The constantly shifting, beautiful pattern of the Louisiana swamplands has been altered by man in a way that, in the long run, may prove shortsighted and disastrous.

The wetlands of the United States, for long regarded as a nuisance, are now being recognized for their true worth. Their contribution to the ecology and beauty of the nation is known, as well as their extensive and beautiful wildlife. The glittering waters of the swamps rank among the finest of America's natural wonders.

DESERTS

In the southwest corner of the State of Maine is a desert. At least the locals say it is a desert. It is true that the colored sand dunes support no life and sweep across many acres. It is also true that the sand is shifting and has buried more than one building in its march to the south. The great Desert of Maine is, however, not a desert at all. Its resemblances to the parched areas of the world are only superficial. For a start it is too small to be more than a large sand pit. Then there is the fact that it rains quite heavily in Maine and the surrounding land is heavily forested. It is not the climate which has created the Desert of Maine, it is the soil. The whole region is a vast area of glacial washout left over from the Ice Ages. It is unusual in that it is so large and that it is so uniformly sandy, without any gravel or soil, but it is by no stretch of the imagination a desert.

Yet the United States does have deserts and it has them in abundance. Great areas of the Southwest are deserts in every sense of the word, with hot and arid climates and an almost complete lack of vegetation. Even more of the continent is covered by scrubby growth which is generally regarded as much a desert as anywhere else. The desert belt extends from the Mexican border northward to beyond the Canadian boundary and is made up of many types of desert with many different names. The arid lands are, however, mainly due to just two climatic factors.

The first affects the southern deserts of Arizona, New Mexico and California and is largely responsible for the Sahara in Africa as well. At the Equator, air is heated by the sun which beats down on the land with an intensity hardly varying throughout the year. This hot air picks up any moisture which might be around and rises high into the atmosphere. At a great height above the earth the hot, moist air cools and swings away to north and to south. At this point the moisture that it picked up precipitates out and falls as rain right across the tropics. These general air movements give rise to the dense stands of jungle which exist in the tropical regions throughout the world. Relieved of its heat and water, the tropical air meets other air currents about the 30° north latitude and begins to descend. The broad band of land which lies around the 30° parallel is constantly kept in the downdraft of these extremely dry air currents. The southwestern states lie around the 30° line and are, therefore, directly in the path of these dry winds. There is not enough water to form clouds and so no rain falls across the Southwestern states. Not only that, but the lack of clouds allows the sun to beat down unmercifully and to burn the deserts beneath its glare.

The more northern deserts of Colorado and Oregon are formed by quite a different pattern of air movements, which are no less far-reaching in their effects. The warm winds which blow off the Pacific are the only winds of the Far West which carry any moisture. Those from any other direction have traveled over vast areas of land where they have deposited their waters long before they reach the Northwestern states. The west winds bring water from the Pacific. Almost the first thing which these moist winds encounter is the great mountain chain of the Rockies. To cross the peaks the air must rise. As it does so it cools down drastically and the water falls as rain or snow upon the mountain tops. It is this effect which gives the phenomenal snowfalls in the western Sierra Nevada; as much as forty feet of snow has been recorded. When the air has crossed the mountains it is bone dry and cannot produce any rain at all. Furthermore, as it descends it warms up, creating hot, dry winds able to dry up any moisture which they may encounter. The combined effect of losing moisture over the mountains and then creating warm winds as the air sweeps down the eastern slopes, is to create large tracts of arid ground to the east of the mountains. This is known as a rain shadow and occurs in several other parts of the world.

A feature of deserts is that there is very little rainfall; indeed there is very little water at all, and this has a marked influence on the scenery. Water is a great erosional influence; one only has to look at the great gash in Arizona which is called the Grand Canyon to realize that. In parts of the nation where there are high levels of rainfall the scenery is gentle and rounded. Any rocks which would have outcropped or formed peaks and mountains are quickly brought down to size. The rugged corners are knocked off and the heights continually worn away to mere stumps. In deserts the situation is quite different and some of the most magnificent and fantastic scenery in the world can result.

Arizona can, at times, be mistaken for one big desert. Though this is far from the truth it has vast areas of desert land and contains some of the finest views in the Southwest. The Colorado River has cut a swath across northern Arizona which has become famous as the largest and most magnificent hole in the ground carved by nature: the Grand Canyon. The sheer, step-like walls of the canyon are due to the lack of rain; too much water would have worn them away to form a wide valley. At the Grand Canyon there is an opposite effect to that in the Sierras. Most people know that it is colder at the top of a mountain than at the bottom, but it may not generally be realized that it is hotter at the base of a canyon than at the rim. Along the rims grow many trees and plants which would be scorched to death in the canyon itself.

But it is not just the Grand Canyon that is a masterpiece of nature among the desert cactus and rose. There is more than one balanced rock within the state. These huge boulders stand precariously poised on tiny bases; often the balance is so fine that they will rock in a strong wind. They are formed by the particular eroding factors found in deserts. Wind-blown sand will blast away at softer rocks and light dews or showers will erode any rocks which are prone to chemical weathering. Where such soft, or erodable, rocks underlie lumps of resistant stone, balancing rocks can easily occur.

In House Rock Valley the sheer heights of the Vermillion Cliffs are one of the wonderful sights which greet the traveler. The rugged, cracked walls live up to their name for, in the blaze of the sun that glares down from the cloudless sky, they shine a fiery red. But even these towering walls are outdone by the beauties revealed to the north at Monument Valley. The fantastic plain, with its dramatic upshot pillars, seems to belong more in fairy land than on the ancient lands of the Navajo. The scene can be viewed from a metalled road, but it takes a hardy vehicle to chance the stony tracks which lead into the valley itself. The great buttes of the area are perhaps the best known of all the desert landmarks for they have featured in more than one John Wayne movie. The numbers of Indians who have bitten the dust around these rocks in the films could not be further removed from the rather peaceful history of the region. The flat-topped crags of the valley are unique and dependent on the desert climate for their very existence. If there was much more rain in the region the sheer columns would have eroded away long ago and the valley would appear as just another plain.

In the Painted Desert alternating bands of different colored rocks have been worn away and exposed to view.

The whole desert earns its name from the contrasting hues of the horizontal bands; hilltops being a quite different color from their bases or even their slopes. Such banding of rock strata achieves an even more remarkable effect in the Mojave Desert. In Red Rock Canyon alternate bands of distinct red and gray rocks, with differing erosion features, give the appearance of delicate Greek pillars supporting roofs of red tiles which rise in terraces to the rim of the canyon.

If the rock features of the southwestern deserts are affected by the climate, so much more so are the plants. The dominating features are the heat and the lack of water. Any plant that is going to survive in desert must make every adaption possible to combat the dryness. For millions of years, generations of plants have been evolving to do just that. The large plants that survive for year after year are designed to take the best advantage of anything that is going. Cacti have tough skins to cut down on evaporation, and are able to store quite large quantities of water within their stems. After the infrequent rains a cactus stem will be distended and almost smooth, but after a long drought the same cactus will be thin and the skin pleated and fluted. The spikes of the cactus are really leaves which have been reduced so much to avoid water loss that they are no longer functional as leaves. Instead they keep would-be herbivores at a distance and safeguard the plant. One species, the twelve-foot tall jumping cholla, uses its spikes to attach seeds to any animal which passes by. Such large plants as the Joshua tree or the saguaro cactus stand some distance apart; the less water there is the further apart they grow. Yet underground the root systems are always just touching. It is as if the plant automatically compensates for the smaller rainfall by spreading over a larger area. Likewise, it seems that other large plants cannot grow where such plants have a root system, too many plants might mean death for them all.

Other plants survive in quite different ways. The ephemerals do not actually live through dry periods at all. When there is rainfall a whole carpet of small plants will spring up across stretches of otherwise barren desert. In a matter of days, they grow, flower and die. Only their seeds remain, scattered across the desert floor waiting for the next fall of rain for their turn to flower and die. Yet other plants have evolved a system of survival which has earned them the name of resurrection plants. These appear to be quite healthy shrubs in times of water, but when the moisture dries up they seem to die much more quickly than any other plant. In fact they do not die at all. What they achieve is a type of suspended animation. They shed any parts of themselves which require fresh water and retain only the shriveled, brown stems where life can be preserved with just the water that they keep stored there. Such plants seem to be quite dead, until the rains come again, sometimes years later, when fresh green shoots break out and the shrub becomes as good as new.

Animals may have an even tougher time in a desert, and the range of animal life is very restricted. Perhaps the most successful are the insects. Like many plants, insects have an impervious skin which retains water and halts evaporation. When the heat and lack of water gets too much insects are able to survive in the form of eggs, much as the seeds of plants perpetuate the species. Ants are famous burrowers and their desert nests are almost always deep underground. It is here that the young are raised and even the adults only leave when it is absolutely necessary. It is hardly surprising that insects are just about the most common animals in any desert.

An animal that certainly appears out of place among the burning wastes is a frog. It needs to pass its tadpole stage in water and to keep its skin wet throughout its life. The truth is that most of the life of a desert amphibian is spent beneath the ground, where it is safe from the heat and dryness. It is only when it rains that the amphibians come out. While the few ponds and streams are full of water, the amphibians mate, lay their eggs and burrow back into the earth. The eggs are left to hatch and develop on their own; only if the water lasts long enough will they mature into adults and burrow down into the ground to join their parents. The life of the desert amphibian is chancy to say the least.

Reptiles are another thing altogether. Their tough, scaly skin cuts down on evaporation and they are probably the most-seen animals in any desert. They feed on insects, amphibians, birds and some are even herbivorous. The sound perpetuated by numerous films and books as one of the most deadly in the desert is the quiet rattle of a reptile. The rattlesnake is a deadly danger to man and any other creature which happens upon it. More often, however, the rattlesnake will quietly slip away from the presence of any large animal. It finds a profitable use for its poison with the animals it preys upon. To a large extent these are the numerous small rodents which manage to survive in the burning heat. The mammals in the desert are nearly all small and are rarely seen in the daytime. They much prefer to come out only at night when it is cool and not much else is active. During the day they stay in burrows or in the shade and it is at this time that they are most vulnerable to the snake. The mobility of the flying birds makes them the most opportunist of the desert animals. As a rule they only fly into the deserts after a fall of rain, when there is plenty of food around. The fleet-footed roadrunner, however, is a very common sight in all the arid lands of the Southwest.

Life in the states near the Mexican border is certainly tough on both animals and plants today, but there is evidence that it was not always so. Giant forests, rich in flora and fauna, once held sway over this land. The shattered remains of these forests can be seen today at Petrified Forest National Park in Arizona. Great logs of stone lie exposed in the rocks and are strewn among the gullies and washouts of the hills. The enormous trees whose trunks form the petrified forest grew some 200 million years ago in the Triassic period, the earliest days of the dinosaurs. When they fell the trees were covered with silt by the dozens of streams which then flowed across the area. Silica seeped into the wood cells and gradually turned to quartz. After millions of years, the rocks containing the petrified trees were uplifted and worn away, exposing the trees to view.

The deserts of the southwest are no longer the lush forests of the Triassic period, but life still moves around beneath the glare of the sun. Up in the Sierra Nevada not much moves at all except the stones. Amid the mountains along the Nevada/California border are many dry playas. These large expanses of dried and caked mud are the beds of long dried up lakes; the rainfall in the desert regions of the hills is not enough to keep the soil damp, let alone keep lakes full. Such dry lake beds are found in many parts of the world, but those of the Sierra Nevada have a mystery which has perplexed man for years. Scattered across the surface of the mud are several large boulders, and the boulders move.

Nobody has actually seen one of the boulders move, but move they do, as much as 800 feet at a time. The stones, some over 600 pounds in weight, do not roll across the playas. They are pushed and leave grooves, or skidmarks, behind them in the dried mud. It was the tracks that pointed the way to the solution of the mystery. It does not rain often up in the mountains, but when it does the waters gush along the usually dry streambeds down to the lakes. When the storms hit the mountains, the waters mix with the mud on the lakebed to create an almost totally frictionless surface. Under such conditions the wind is quite capable of sliding the boulders along. Though the secret of the moving stones has been solved, it is still an eerie sight to see a huge, heavy boulder which has moved hundreds of yards, seemingly under its own power.

The playas which sport the moving stones are high up in the mountains, but they are still included in the Death Valley National Monument. The valley itself is one of the most remarkable natural features of the country. It is 140 miles long, 15 miles wide and, in places, 280 feet below sea level. The weather in the valley is phenomenal, with temperatures of over 120°F not at all unusual.

The valley gained its gruesome name from a group of settlers who crossed it in 1849 and suffered greatly from its heat and lack of water, but it was already millions of years old by that time. During the Oligocene period great faults opened up in the earth's crust in western America. At Death Valley the faulting resulted in both the sinking of the valley floor and the raising of the surrounding hills. The valley is continuing to sink even today and is several inches deeper than it was when the settlers crossed it.

Today, the valley is touched by a main route from Las Vegas to Los Angeles. The many travelers along the route can get a taste of the valley's scenery around the aptly-named town of Baker. Few people make the trip into Death Valley itself and there are even fewer roads. It is hardly surprising that so few take the risk of entering the valley for it is still claiming victims today and the scenery, though spectacular, is hardly beautiful. The ground was once measured to be a stunning 190°F in temperature and the idea of water freezing in the valley is almost unthinkable. Not only is it never that cold, but the rainfall averages out at less that 2 inches a year. It is not unknown for several years to pass without any rain falling at all. Death Valley has not always been the furnace that it is today. During the Ice Ages the depression was filled with water to a depth of some 600 feet and animal life abounded around the shores of the lake. The conditions for life have changed drastically. In summer it is estimated that the average human will sweat away 2 pints of water every hour just trying to keep cool. Even so, some of the hardier forms of life have found a place in the valley.

Far to the east, over the Sangre de Cristo Range of mountains lies an area of desert which is probably more like the average person's idea of what a desert should look like. The Great Sand Dunes National Monument has been created around a series of mighty sand dunes which reach up to a thousand feet in height. The huge area of shifting waves of sand stands in the San Luis Valley. The beautiful white sands, which stand out in contrast to the dark mountains beyond, were formed by the winds which howl down the valleys and through the mountains. They carry with them large quantities of eroded rock and sand which are dumped at the Great Sand Dunes, where the wind eddies and slows. Unlike the burning wastes of Death Valley, the rolling hills of sand are easily reached on State Highway 17 and, therefore, receive thousands of visitors every year.

On the eastern slopes of the Oregon mountains is a vast plateau of ancient lava which has been turned into a desert by the rain shadow effect of the western mountains. This is a land where trees will not grow, and the few plants that can survive cling to the bare hillsides. The eruptions of volcanoes now long dead have scattered fantastic shapes across the face of the desert. One of these, the Devil's Thumb at Leslie Gulch, is a towering column of rock which stands free of the surrounding scrub desert. Like Death Valley, the rainshadow deserts of the eastern slopes were once awash with water. At Dry Falls, in the Washington desert, a sheer rock face stands in mute testimony to what may have been America's largest waterfall. The end of the Ice Ages was marked by shifting drainage patterns and rivers which altered their courses. It was at this time that the Niagara Falls were created. But in the west the flood waters from the glaciers poured over a plateau edge in a cataract 400 feet high and nearly 4 miles across.

America may be a vast and fertile land, but its deserts occupy large areas and contribute much to the scenery and grandeur of the nation.

COASTS

The very first part of the United States to be seen by any of the early European settlers was its coast. Though this was, and still is, one of the most beautiful parts of the Eastern states, it was surprisingly neglected by many of the early settlers. Yet the coasts of America are not only among its great scenic splendors, they are also among its most productive areas.

The voyages of Columbus, which publicized the existence of a great continent to the west, paved the way for merchants, adventurers and kings to spread to the New World. But Columbus' voyage had been preceded centuries earlier by the Vikings. Unlike the more fortunate Columbus, who came upon lush islands and tales of gold, the Vikings only found a cold shore and hostile Indians. Their attempts at colonization were short-lived and the record of the Western continent was soon lost in the sagas and relegated to the realms of imaginative folklore. Prompted by the rich Spanish discoveries to the south, the English sent out John Cabot on a voyage on a more northerly route. He discovered something, though where he made his landfall on the North American coast is still disputed because his log was so inaccurate. It was on the basis of this voyage that England, the deadly enemy of Spain, based her claims on North America.

Nearly a hundred years after John Cabot disappeared in the mists of the Atlantic, another Englishman was sailing the coasts of America. Sir Francis Drake, however, was in the Pacific with his ship full of plundered Spanish gold. He came across the inviting California shores and claimed the land for his Queen. Having set up a plaque to substantiate his claim, Drake sailed away again. Despite all this claiming of territory, no Englishman had, as yet, actually gotten around to living in America.

That came on the East coast of America at Roanoke Island. In 1587 the colony disappeared and another thirty years passed before the first successful colony was founded at Jamestown. Even so, it was not the bountiful coast that drew men to the New World, it was land. Anyone who could afford to get to Virginia was given fifty acres of land on the spot. So the settlers came and farmed the land. Meanwhile, to the north the rich Newfoundland Banks were being harvested of their fish by some of the bolder fishermen of Europe who came over by way of Iceland. It was not long before the New Englanders realized that their shoreline had more to offer than just beauty.

The Puritans of Massachusetts were the first to take to fishing along the coasts. Even today the fish cuisine of Boston is undisputed, a cuisine based upon the abundant sea life. Living right on the rocky coastline of New England itself is the clam. There are many types of clam and perhaps the best known is the quahog. This little creature can be picked up almost anywhere in the tidal zone of the beautiful coastline. Baked and served with bread and butter, there are few better seafoods. One of the rare delicacies which is better than a good

American quahog is the lobster, and these are found off the New England coast as well. The American lobster, *Homarus americanus*, is acknowledged as one of the tastiest species. When caught, lobsters usually weigh around five pounds, but some have been known to grow to a size of forty pounds in deeper water. But of all the seafoods connected with Massachusetts in general, and Boston in particular, perhaps the most universal is the cod. Bostonians know a hundred different ways to dish up this tasty, if unassuming, fish.

The fact that there is such an abundance of delicious seafood off the coast of Eastern North America has nothing at all to do with the fact that Puritans came to live there some three and a half centuries ago. It is the result of sea currents and land formations which date back thousands, if not millions of years.

Stretching along the eastern coast of America, from the Mexican to the Canadian borders is a huge geological feature known as the Coastal plain. This vast platform, which covers thousands of square miles, has had a greatly varied history. As the sea level rises and falls it has been alternately flooded and exposed. At the moment, the majority of it is under water and forms the Continental Shelf, a stretch of shallow water which may reach as much as 250 miles out to sea. The forms and diversity of the Coastal Plain, be it dry land or seabed, are the controlling factors of the Eastern and Southern coasts of America.

North of the city of New York, the layered, sedimentary rocks of the Coastal Plain take a very definite downturn and plunge beneath the waters of the Atlantic. Almost the whole width of the Coastal Plain is below the ocean in New England. This means that the waters and waves of the rolling Atlantic beat directly upon the jagged, warped rocks of the Appalachians. The rocky and dramatic coast of the Northeast owes far more to the titanic forces which threw up the mountains than to anything else.

It is on the shores of New England that the coastline is at its most picturesque. Tree-fringed cliffs rise above the fog-covered waves and this is the area to find the rock-bound tidal pool and the shingle beach. Though it is not as attractive to the vacationer as a sweep of golden sand, the pebbles are just as lovely. The individual stones have been worn by time and the crashing waves produce a slurping, rattling sound that is found on no other beaches in America. The mountain-backed shore of rock affected the wildlife of the region, creating a unique community of animals. It is these animals which grace the tables of seafood lovers the world over.

The coast of Maine shows the effects of the Appalachian building forces clearer than most. The sea beats directly onto the folded rocks of the mountains and pushes its fingers into the land in a series of long, thin bays. The bays are directed north to south and are separated by long peninsulas of tough, jagged rocks. The forces which thrust up the mountains folded them into a series of ridges and valleys which ran in a north to south direction. Over the millions of years which have passed since their formation, the once huge peaks have been worn down and the valleys gouged out by grinding glaciers. The peninsulas and promontories of Maine reflect the geological history of the region, with its folding and cracking, far removed from the flat, stable formations of the Coastal Plain rocks.

The first signs of the Coastal Plain to be seen above the ocean surface, indeed the only visible parts of the plain in New England, are the islands of Nantucket and Martha's Vineyard and the hooked peninsula of Cape Cod. At once the scenery is dramatically different from the rock-bound shores of Maine and New Hampshire. The coasts hereabouts, as every vacationer knows, are broad, sandy and beautiful. If the beaches have lost the splintered magnificence of the north, they have gained immeasurably in the things people look for. The sandy beaches are ideal to bathe from and the sand dunes are ready-made playgrounds for anyone who wants to make use of them. The two islands and Cape Cod itself are, strictly speaking, not really part of the Coastal Plain at all. They are formations of land built up by glaciers just a few thousand years ago. The grinding glaciers, which carved out the bays of Maine, dumped their accumulated debris on the Coastal Plain in giant mounds. It is these mounds which actually break the surface of the Atlantic, but they indicate the presence of the Coastal Plain as it rises towards the surface.

South of the glacial sands which form Cape Cod, the Coastal Plain continues to rise and begins to form a strip of land between the ocean and the Appalachians. Though as it travels south the Coastal Plain rises progressively above the level of the sea, it is still much lower than it has been in the past. The rivers of the East Coast once flowed out across lowlands which now form the sea bed. The valleys which the rivers carved in those distant days have now been flooded by the sea and form wide bays and inlets. Perhaps the most beautiful of these drowned valleys, or rias as they are known, is Chesapeake Bay. The bay, which is the largest on the East Coast, was formed when the valley of the Susquehanna River disappeared under the rising sea water following the end of the last Ice Age. With the Susquehanna Valley went the Potomac, Rappahannock and Nanticoke river valleys. The western shore of the bay is a definite shoreline between ocean and land, demarcated by cliffs and hills. The eastern shores are quite different: here, the coast is a network of irregular headlands and bays backed by low, marshy land whose contours are continually shifting.

The accident of its formation and the sheltered waters it contains have long made Chesapeake Bay vitally important to the development of the United States. It was into the safe anchorages of the bay that the early settlers came in 1607. They established the first city in Virginia and the upper reaches of the bay were later chosen as the site of the nation's capital. But two centuries after the first Englishman landed at Jamestown, the British returned to the bay and burned the city of Washington to the ground. Since the War of 1812 the bay has increased in importance, becoming the trade outlet for the great port of Baltimore.

South of Norfolk, Virginia, the Coastal Plain becomes even more apparent above the waves. A broad stretch of flatland extends from the Appalachians for nearly two hundred miles before it reaches the ocean. The land is drained by many rivers which run parallel to each other in a southwest direction. They do not do a very good job and much land is lost to the swamps and marshes of the area. Albemarle and Pamlico Sounds are, like Chesapeake Bay, inundated river valleys. Unlike the bay to the north, they have never been particularly important. This fact can probably be attributed to the remarkable coasts of the sounds. Far beyond the coast proper lies a line of banks which almost cut the sounds off from the open ocean and which effectively prevent any large ship from entering them. A combination of ocean currents, sediment-laden rivers and the relief of the ocean bed has conspired to make the North Carolina coast an ideal place to dump sand and sediment. The long, low islands of sand make for fantastic surfing beaches and Carolina does have some of the best seaside resorts in the nation. Those same sand dunes and peculiar winds made conditions ideal for a pair of bicycle makers who wanted to try out their new invention. In 1903 the Wright brothers finally got their powered airplane into the air at Kitty Hawk, near Albemarle Sound.

The shifting sands make the coastline treacherous for modern ships, but the small vessels of the sixteenth century found sheltered waters inside Oregon Inlet. The fine land of Roanoke Island lies just behind Bodie Island and was the site of the famous lost colony of Englishmen. While their native land faced invasion from the Spanish Armada, the lonely souls of England's first American colony died on an unfriendly shore. Today, the island is the site of the much more successful town of Manteo and receives its fair share of visitors, who come to see the site of the lost colony.

One thing has not changed about the Carolina coastline since the days of Sir Walter Raleigh and that is the abundance of bird life. Cape Hatteras has over 350 species of wild birds frequenting its shores. The island offers a number of natural habitats: dunes, saltmarsh, mudflats and open sea. All through the year migratory and resident birds congregate at Cape Hatteras in enormous numbers. Hundreds of migrating snow geese and other waterfowl swoop down on the islands, only to disappear as suddenly as they arrive. The true wonders of coastal wildlife, however, are found much further to the south.

The broad geological feature of the Coastal Plain rises increasingly above the surface as the coastline tends southward. South of the 32nd parallel the Coastal Plain rises up to form a long, low hump. In the scale of geological features the rise in the plain is almost unnoticeable. Beside the towering heights of the Rockies, for example, it is not much more than a molehill. Yet the rise in the land is one of the most significant features of the East Coast: Florida. Nowhere in the entire peninsula does the land rise more than 350 feet above the sea and much of it is barely dry land at all.

Large areas of the coast are no more than ten feet above the surface of the ocean. This makes the coast of Florida dangerously vulnerable to the fierce Atlantic storms. The mighty rollers sweep down upon the coast and crash against the shoreline with tremendous force. They are a fact of life in the southern state and would be a great erosional force on the coast if it were not for a plant. The mangroves of the coast are a peculiar plant. They are among the very few land plants which have been able to take to salt water in a big way. The roots of a mangrove branch out and are immensely strong. They take a firm hold on the mud underlying the shallow coast and grow upwards. The plant then produces more stems and roots which create a tangle of vegetation that is impossible to penetrate. A really dense stand of mangroves can reach right along a shoreline and trap the shifting mud and sand of the shallows. The stabilized mud increases in area and depth as more and more mud is trapped, until it eventually becomes dry land. It is the impenetrable forest of mangrove stems and roots which has held the sea at bay so effectively along much of the low-lying coast.

Off the extreme southern tip of Florida is an area of some 800 square miles of sea where the seabed is never more than ten feet below the surface. This is the great Florida Bay, which forms part of the Everglades National Park. It is a fascinating place where the line between land and sea is blurred so much as to almost disappear. There are more than a hundred keys in the bay, but some are little more than mudflats which have poked their heads above water. It is in the bay that the effects of the mangroves can be seen at their most spectacular. Nearly all the islands are held together by mangroves, otherwise they would break up and drift away. In other places marine grasses are the dominant plant. Turtle Grass has flat leaves up to two feet long, while Manatee Grass has cylindrical leaves of about the same length. Unlike the sturdy mangroves, the marine grasses are vulnerable to attack by the forces of nature.

Within the bay lives one of the strangest of America's coastal animals: the manatee. The curious manatee, known to some as the sea cow, is one of the oldest of America's mammals. It has hardly changed since it first evolved some 45 million years ago during the Eocene period. They are fairly large animals, about eight feet long, and rank with the most sluggish of all mammals. A heavy animal with solid bones and rather weak muscles, its main form of locomotion is to gently beat its semi-circular tail in the water. The broad front flippers only come in useful for steering. This gentle, inoffensive animal spends most of its time browsing on the water plants of the area. There are no predators in the shallows capable of feeding on the manatee and its only enemy is the motorboat, which moves so quickly that no manatee has a chance of getting out of the way in time.

Off Key Largo, in the eastern part of the bay, is an underwater state park. The John Pennekamp Coral Reef State Park, as its name suggests, was created to preserve the wonderful coral reef which grows off Key Largo. The coral reef is an incredible natural formation of great beauty. Millions of tiny coral polyps each build up a skeleton of limestone to protect themselves and when they die the skeleton is added to the reef. It takes millions of generations to build up a reef the size of that at Key Largo and conditions have to be exactly right for the polyp to thrive. In most places the water is too cold or too deep or too dirty for the tiny animals to survive; that is why reefs are so rare around the American coast. In the tropical wonderland off the Florida coast live a multitude of brilliantly colored fish and a unique range of flora. In the deeper waters live the marlin and sailfish so beloved by big game fishermen.

To the west of Florida the Coastal Plain slopes back beneath the surface of the waves. A broad shelf of rock stretches out from the peninsula into the Gulf of Mexico and all the way to Texas and Mexico. West of Cape San Blas the coast loses much of its low-lying swamp character, only to pick it up again beyond the Chandeleur Islands.

Just as Florida is a rise in the underlying rocks, this region represents a dip in their normally level structure. But instead of there being a deep embayment, the coastline sweeps outwards to form a large peninsula which ends at South Pass. In fact, left to itself, the Coastal Plain would have created a long, thin inlet which would have reached as far north as Tennessee. The rivers of the Mississippi Basin, however, had other ideas. For millions of years they have been been washing sediments down from the north and dumping the soils and sediments around their mouths. These have managed to fill the shallow inlet with enough debris to raise it above sea level.

Today the process of land reclamation by the Mississippi is still continuing and creates a unique coast in Louisiana. The shifting marshes, banks and channels of the Mississippi Delta form a wonderful refuge for wildlife and a precious heritage which is of vital importance to the state.

West of the delta stretches the Texas coastline. With its offshore sand bars, islands and lagoons, the coast of Texas is somewhat similar to that of North Carolina. The offshore islands of sand and sediment form a home for wildlife every bit as rich as the Louisiana swamps. It is here that the whooping crane maintains its last outpost in the wild. Fewer than a hundred of the magnificent birds are still alive, but even that is twice as many as there were in 1951. Alligators vie with the stunning bird life of the islands for the accolade of the most important inhabitant of the offshore islands, which are rich in insect and amphibian life as well. The great diversity of life to be found on the islands has existed for thousands of years, but the oil business is beginning to encroach on the native wildlife. In 1979 a test well off Mexico blew, and oil swept up the coast, bringing death in its wake. Luckily such events are rare and the oil companies are taking conservation seriously.

The Coastal Plain which has such a dominant effect upon the East Coast is entirely absent from the West Coast. Instead of a wide, stable slab of rock the West Coast is dominated by the mountains. The line of the coast is dependent upon the great forces which created the Western Cordillera. The Coast Ranges have a complicated geological history which is intricately bound up with that of the Rockies and the infamous San Andreas Fault.

The California coast is reminiscent of the coast of Maine, but far more spectacular. There are rocky headlands and surf smashed boulders, but in the south there are stretches of sandy beaches. The Santa Monica Mountains stand back from the sea and allow the coast around Los Angeles to form a great crescent of sand from Palos Verdes to Malibu. Further north the Big Sur is as wild and far from civilization as it is possible to get. Cliffs plunge down into the sea where the mountains sweep right down to the shore.

North of the entrance to the great bay of San Francisco is a granite peninsula of great beauty: Point Reyes. It was named *Punta de los Reyes*, the Point of Kings, by the Spaniards but the name has been changed by later settlers to better fit the American language. There are tall cliffs where sea birds swoop and call in their endless search for fish, and there are secluded beaches where seals can bask and breed. It was the cliffs and sands that gained California its first name, that of Nova Albion. Sir Francis Drake stopped off here after plundering the Spanish colonies of Mexico of their gold. He was struck by the resemblance of the coast to that of Sussex in England, so it was only natural that he should give the land a name which translates as "New England". The title, however, was later usurped by an area at the other end of the continent.

As the coast stretches north it becomes increasingly rugged and scenic. In places the mountains crowd right up to the sea and cliffs far taller than those seen by Drake drop down into the surf. Isolated stacks of rock stand far out into the ocean marking the sites of ancient promontories which have not yet been completely worn away by the pounding ocean. At other spots the waves have worn away at weak spots and undercut the rock. Natural arches are as much a feature of the rugged, mountain-backed shore as they are of the southwestern deserts.

The coast becomes more and more isolated from human contact as it moves further from the great cities of California. In 1592 a Greek captain of a Spanish ship was sailing along this coast when he found a channel leading into the continent. Nobody is quite sure what he found, but it was probably Juan de Fuca Strait. If it was not, then the strait has been misnamed for the Greek's name was Juan de Fuca. Whatever the intrepid captain discovered he was the first European to touch upon the shores of what is now the northwestern boundary of the conterminous United States. He marveled at the forest-covered slopes that reached down to the sea. The islands of San Juan were almost the cause of a war with Britain in 1859, or rather a pig was. The ownership of the nations was still disputed at the time and settlers from both islands had arrived. In that year an American shot a pig which belonged to a Briton and then offered to pay for it. The Briton, however, started legal proceedings against the American who refused to recognize a British Court. Before long five hundred Americans were armed and ready for war, despite the fact that they were faced by 2,000 Britons. It was only the arrival of the British Admiral Byers which calmed tempers and defused the situation. It was not until 1870 that Britain recognized America's ownership of the islands and pulled back to Canada.

The coasts of America were the first parts of the nation to be settled and are still among the most beautiful areas of the country. They produce shellfish and contain a wealth of wildlife which is an important part of the American natural heritage.

GREAT PLAINS

If there is one scene which epitomizes the American frontiersman it is that of a buckskin-clad figure fighting off hordes of whooping redskins as they close in on a wagon train of settlers. The picture may not be quite true and Indian fights occured across the country from Virginia and Florida to Arizona and California, but it is the Plains which are recognized as the center of the great Indian Wars. It was on the Plains that General Custer was massacred along with his entire command, and here that the settlers actually settled down to some serious farming.

The immense area which comprises the Great Plains has had a long geological history. For approaching 600 million years nothing very much has happened to the tough, crystalline rocks which underlie the central states. While the Appalachians were thrown up and ground away in the East, and when the mighty Rockies and Cascades erupted from the earth in the West, the central block of rock did nothing. Far to the north the Canadian Shield, north of the Great Lakes, is an area where the ancient rocks are laid bare at the surface and are revealed for all to see. But across the immensity of the Great Plains the solid rocks are not to be seen. Millions of years ago the sea invaded the central states and separated the western and eastern edges of the continent. On the bed of the vast, shallow sea that was formed, thick bands of sedimentary rocks were laid down. It is these layered rocks which form the Great Plains today.

The plains are quite simply enormous. They cover more than a million square miles and seem endless to anyone traveling across them. They may be known as vast sweeps of grassland, but the Plains have a varied landscape. In the Texas Panhandle they are dead flat, so flat that it is well known that you can lie on your belly and see for miles. It is equally well known that there isn't anything much to see. The Black Hills of South Dakota, on the other hand, are tree-covered hills several hundred feet higher than the surrounding plains. Apart from the Panhandle, the Great Plains are not as flat as they are generally thought to be. In Colorado, where they meet the Rockies, the Plains are some 5,000 feet above sea level. At their eastern boundary the same plains are just 1,500 feet high. They appear so flat because there is such a vast distance between the two and because there are few, if any, hills in between.

The prairies spread across much of central North America and have a continental type of climate. In summer the weather can become almost unbearably hot as the sun beats down upon the shadeless land. As winter draws in the snows begin to fall and the temperatures plummet. By January the Plains are in the grip of possibly the most severe weather in America. The reason for the drastic difference between the seasons is simply the fact that the Plains are so far from the ocean. Seas remain at a pretty constant temperature throughout the year and exert a moderating effect on the weather of coastal regions. Land, on the other hand, can heat up and cool down rapidly and the ground temperature varies with that of the air. Any place which is distant from the sea, as most of the Great Plains are, will have wildly fluctuating temperatures.

The temperatures in themselves are not sufficient to explain why the Plains are taken up by sweeping panoramas of grass, and not by dense stands of forest. The climatic conditions which have closed the land to forest have more to do with rainfall, and that too is dependent upon the Plains' location on the continent. Rainfall is brought by water-laden winds, and winds can only pick up water by passing over wide stretches of ocean. Any winds which come from the Pacific lose their rain as they pass over the towering Rockies. Likewise the rain from the east is caught by the Appalachians before it can reach the Plains. The only route open to moisture-bearing air is from the south. Winds from that direction have only been able to pass over the Gulf of Mexico, which is not a particularly large body of water, and so do not hold as much rain as they might. The result of the wind pattern is that the Plains receive low amounts of rainfall. The southern plains of Texas, which lie nearest to the Gulf of Mexico, can expect some 20 inches of water to fall each year, while the open spaces of Nebraska, far to the north, are lucky if they get 13 inches in the same space of time. It is this lack of rainfall which has resulted in the total absence of forest and the predominance of grass in the landscape. Unfortunately the rainfall seems to come in cycles, a fact which would lead to much suffering among the early settlers.

Grass is a remarkable plant. It can grow almost unbelievably quickly after having been eaten right down to its roots. Under favorable conditions, such as exist on the Great Plains, it can provide an endless source of food for any animal which has teeth strong enough to deal with the tough grass stalks. For millions of years the plains have been the home of vast numbers of grazing animals and of their predators.

Nearly forty million years ago a small creature, no more than two feet tall, was roaming the plains, munching away at the waving grass. *Mesohippus*, as it is now called, had batteries of strong, ridged teeth well able to grind down the tough grass and it could run fast enough to escape almost any predator. The animal flourished and evolved until by 2 million years ago it had become the horse. The wild horse is superbly adapted to life on the plains. It can outrun almost anything and has a digestive system which makes short work of the grass. As the Pleistocene period opened, some 2 million years ago, the plains were dominated by vast herds of horses and of pronghorns, of which there were then dozens of different species. During the Pleistocene period a land bridge opened up between Alaska and Asia and the animals from both continents were able to mingle and migrate. What followed is most curious. The horse moved over into Asia and thence into Europe while the buffalo spread in the opposite direction. The horse then promptly became extinct in its native North America, but continued to flourish in its new home of Eurasia. The buffalo proceeded to take over the grasslands of America, pushing the pronghorns to the edge of extinction, but did rather badly in its native land of Asia.

When the first settlers brought horses to America, the Indians did not know what to make of the strange neighing beasts. The wide open spaces of the west belonged to the buffalo and there were something like sixty million of the animals at the start of the last century. A good buffalo could weigh anywhere up to 1,500 pounds; more if it belonged to the woods buffalo subspecies. It was, like most members of the cattle family, a ready made source of tasty meat and the Indians weren't slow to exploit this great natural resource. They used to drive whole herds of buffalo over the edges of cliffs, chasing them with fire and on foot. The Indians would then take what they needed in the way of meat, bones and hides and leave the rest of the buffalo herd to rot. It was the horse which ushered in the heyday of buffalo hunting, for it represented a more select way of killing.

Instead of slaughtering whole herds, the Indians could now keep up with the thundering buffalo and only kill what they actually needed, leaving the rest of the herd for another time. The acquisition of the horse from neighboring tribes, who had taken them from the white man, gave the plains tribes a decided edge in battle. Warfare flared up with fresh ferocity across the plains as the great tribes of Sioux and Cheyenne embarked on relentless wars to drive their weaker neighbors off the best hunting grounds. It was into this land of war and buffalo hunting that the first white man arrived in the early years of the nineteenth century.

Strangely enough, the first white men to come to the Great Plains were actually mountain men. The longhaired, bearded men penetrated the Rockies in search of beaver and other valuable pelt animals. They only really came across the Plains because they were in the way. The same reason brought the first wagon trains across the Plains in the 1830s. Twelve thousand pioneers traveled the Oregon Trail in 1848 and the flood of settlers, even though they were just passing through, began to anger the Indians. Trouble began quietly enough with an occasional theft, flared temper and shooting, but in the 1850s the wars began in earnest.

It is the wars with the Plains Indians which have captured the popular imagination. Hordes of whooping redskins have swept across many a film screen in pursuit of a stagecoach or ringing an isolated cabin. Such raiding tactics were typical of the Indian wars and major battles were rare. It was the incursion of the white man which started the trouble, and the killing of the buffalo on which the Indians relied which increased it, but it was gold which led to the greatest Indian victory of the wars and to their eventual defeat.

In the early 1870s rumors of gold in the Black Hills began to seep out and hundreds of prospectors poured into the lands which had been guaranteed to the Indians in a treaty of 1868. First the American government tried to stop the prospectors, then it tried to buy the land from the Indians. Neither side would budge and war broke out again. In June, 1876, as part of a coordinated attack, General George Armstrong Custer led his 7th Cavalry into Indian territory. Within a few days he and half his regiment were dead and the Indians had achieved their greatest victory. But they had used up most of their ammunition and within a year the last significant force of Indians on the plains had surrendered and gone onto reservations. Later trouble was as nothing compared to the wars of the '60s and '70s. The Indian problem was solved.

With the Indians out of the way the Great Plains were wide open to the settlers. The hardy pioneers were set to exploit the Plains, just as the Indians had, but the white men had the knowledge and equipment to do it far better. The first resource of the Plains to feel the brunt of the white man's attentions was the animal population. The sixty million buffalo of 1800 were not to survive for long. Buffalo robes commanded high prices back East and buffalo tongue rapidly became a noted delicacy. There was big money to be made out of hunting buffalo and the buffalo themselves were particularly helpful about being shot. Unlike most game animals, the buffalo would not stampede at the sight of a man. They would not even run when the sound of a rifle shot split the air. When a dedicated buffalo hunter came across a herd of the magnificent beasts he could carry on shooting them until his bullets ran out. The hunter would then take the hide and tongue of the buffalo and leave the rest of the carcass to rot on the prairie.

By 1883 the last of the big herds had been wiped out and by 1900 only 20 buffalo remained in the wild. Fortunately, several private individuals had kept groups of the once all-powerful bovines and these were gradually brought together to form the basis of a breeding stock. Today, there are several areas of the United States where buffalo can be seen roaming free; one of these is the National Bison Range in Montana. The herd of some 500 buffalo on the range owes its origins to Walking Coyote of the Pend d'Oreille Indian tribe. In 1873 Walking Coyote went hunting with other men from his tribe and brought back four young buffalo alive. The descendants of these animals formed the 34 buffalo which, with seven others, became the ancestors of the range's herd. Though the buffalo may never again wander the Great Plains in the millions that they once did, the survival of the species has been assured by the maintenance of such herds as that at Moiese, Montana. North of the Canadian border a herd of the rare woods buffalo has been protected and bred. The woods buffalo subspecies was never common, but grew to a much larger size than the ordinary plains buffalo, weights of 2,600 pounds being far from rare.

The demise of the buffalo herds opened up vast areas of plains for the exploitation by man. The grass was no longer being eaten by the buffalo, so it was up to the white man to find a use for it. In 1493 Columbus arrived in America on his second voyage of discovery and he brought with him a number of cattle. Later Spanish settlers brought even more. By 1700 the Spaniards had crossed the Rio Grande into what is now Texas, bringing their cattle with them. The grazing land of Texas was sparse and the cattle hardy. Over the years the once domestic cattle became wilder and wilder as they adapted to surviving in their new and unfriendly environment. It was from these half-wild Spanish cattle that the great Texas longhorn developed.

At the close of the Civil War the Southern States were devastated, but the plains of Texas had a valuable commodity: beef. The cities of the North and East were crying out for good, cheap meat and the Plains were the ideal place to graze stock. The bitter winter and poor grazing would have killed off most breeds of cattle around at the time, but not the longhorn. Within a few decades the longhorn had replaced the buffalo across great reaches of the plains. There were millions of the cattle on the Great Plains and the market for them seemed inexhaustible. In 1871 alone, more than half a million traveled the Chisholm Trail north from Texas. By 1895 the Texas longhorn began to give up the Plains just as the buffalo had some years earlier. There were more men to manage the herds and it was found that with the right amount of care whitefaced cattle would survive. Whitefaced cattle gave better beef and commanded higher prices at the railhead. It was soon more profitable to run the new breed on fenced pasture and employ more men than to keep the semi-wild longhorn. By 1920 the great longhorn was almost extinct, again it was individuals who saved the breed from extinction. The western writer J. Frank Dobie bought a small herd of the cattle which had helped make him rich and decided to conserve them. That herd flourished and today it is owned and managed by the Texas State Government at the Fort Griffin State Park. Only those animals which are true to the breed are kept for breeding, the rest are sold off at auction.

Even after the longhorn had largely disappeared from the Plains, the life of the hardworking cowboy continued much as before. He would spend his time rounding up steers, branding them and breaking horses much as he had since the demise of the buffalo. The life of the cowboy on the Great Plains is as much a legend as the Indian wars. He has come to represent a side of the American character which has never quite disappeared. The self-reliant, rugged individualist of the open prairies is an important force in American history. But the actual days of the cowboys themselves were remarkably short. The cattle took over from the buffalo in the 1870s and the farmer took over from the rancher in the 1890s. If the Stetson-wearing, gunslinging cowboy is the image of the Great Plains that Hollywood and numerous writers would have us remember, the modern traveler gains a quite different picture. The vast, empty reaches of the "big sky country" are still there, and the rolling plains still sway with grass. Today, however, the grass is cultivated grass in the form of wheat. The endless panorama is broken by fences and roads. The vast prairies have at last been tamed and man has left a permanent mark on the huge area of the West.

The first farmers came to the prairies when the cattlemen still ruled supreme. The government allowed anyone to claim a 160 acre plot simply by settling down on it. Naturally the new farmers, most of them direct from Europe, settled on the best land near the rivers. This cut off the water from the great herds of the cattlemen. The cattle owners were not the kind of men to watch their herds, and their fortunes, die off because of a few homesteaders. Many small farmers were forced to move on, but others refused to move. In Wyoming, in 1892, tempers finally boiled over. The cattle owners hired fifty gunslingers from Texas to deal with the most truculent homesteaders, a death-list of about 30 names being prepared. When the gunmen arrived, they only managed to kill one man before they were soundly beaten by 200 armed farmers. The famous Johnson County War gained nobody anything and only served to heighten tension.

Eventually, of course, the farmers won by sheer force of numbers, and the fact that they could produce far more from an acre of land than a rancher could. The small farmsteader brought with him the metal plow, and it was that simple tool which spelled the end of the prairie landscape of the Great Plains. The steel plow could cut through the heavy, rich soil with ease. Once plowed the land became lighter and better aerated, making conditions ideal for growing wheat. But the weather remained a problem for the first farmers. The bitter winters and short growing season made life difficult for the strains of wheat then available. It wasn't until fresh waves of settlers arrived from the steppes of Eastern Europe that a strain of wheat was introduced which could prosper on the Great Plains. Farming blossomed and the smallholder ruled the Plains.

But the Great Plains had one last surprise in store for the men who tried to tame them. The years since the first farmers arrived had been rainy for the Plains. Many more inches of water fell to nourish the soil than was normal. It was this heavy rainfall that the settlers took for normal conditions. When the true normal conditions returned, the folly of the farmers was revealed. Drought gripped the land and crops withered under the scorching sun. Intensively grazed stock were suddenly left with insufficient water and began to die in enormous numbers. Far worse than the failing crops and the skinny cattle was the effect that the steel plow had on the very soil. The processes of aeration and lightening had made the soil dangerously susceptible to such drought as arrived. The soil was no longer tightly-packed and there were no strong grass roots to hold the ground in place. When the sun killed the crops there was nothing to bind the soil; when the hot winds blew they were able to take the soil with them. Vast areas of the once-lush plains became huge dustbowls in a single season and worse was to come.

The great fertile heartland of America almost disappeared into desert. Families left the land and whole communities simply ceased to exist. The population of the plains dropped by a third and was only saved from further decimation by the prosperity of industry in the towns. It looked as if man had not only wantonly destroyed the buffalo which grazed on the prairies but was also in the process of destroying the whole tremendous area of the Great Plains themselves.

Luckily, new agricultural techniques were developed and the dustbowls were brought back to the fertile land they had been before. Today, large farms have replaced the inefficent smallholdings of pre-dustbowl years. Crops including wheat, sorghum, hay and cotton and livestock continue to be important products of the Great Plains. Careful management has made the Great Plains of the United States into the breadbasket of the world. The sweeps of the rolling plains have changed from the haunt of buffalo and Indian, to the home of longhorn and cowboy, to the realm of the homesteader, until today it is the province of big business in the form of large, economic farms. But the old prairie is beginning to stage something of a comeback, with a little help from man.

The ecosystem of the prairie was immensely complicated, with dozens of plants and animals cooperating in the smooth running of the environment. It is the tallgrass prairie which is benefiting most from the efforts of conservationists. The beautiful waving stands of grass once covered parts of Texas, Oklahoma, Arkansas, Kansas, Missouri, Tennessee, Kentucky, Ohio, Indiana, Michigan, Illinois, Nebraska, Iowa, Minnesota, both Dakotas and reached well into Canada. Today, pitifully few stands of the majestic tallgrass remain, and most of these are less than a hundred acres in extent. But the people who live on the land are becoming more aware of the value of grass which can stand more than six feet tall and hide a man with great ease. The reddish grass of the natural prairie is showing through the imported plants in many preserves across the nation. Prairie grasses have deeper and stronger roots than any foreign strains, even wheat, and given a fair chance soon outstrip any other plants. It will not be long before the buffalo will be able to graze on the native tallgrass again in a special 320,000-acre park. They may not spread as far as they once did, but some approximation to the natural Great Plains will remain.

ALASKA

Until little more than a century ago Russia owned a sizeable chunk of North America. Alaska only became part of the United States in 1868 and was not admitted to the Union, as the 49th state, until 1959. The story of its half million square miles dates back several hundred years, perhaps to the time of the first settlers on the East Coast.

By the year 1700 the rapidly expanding Russian Empire had pushed its borders to the easternmost reaches of Asia. The natives of Eastern Siberia had long been fishermen and put out into the cold North Pacific in their frail craft in search of fish. On occasion the vagaries of the weather pushed the Siberians further east than they intended to go and there they saw a wondrous sight. Tales soon drifted back to the court of the Tsar of the fabulous land lying to the east of his newly-acquired territories in Asia. Always eager for new lands to occupy and exploit, the Tsar commissioned an expedition to discover just what was really out in the Pacific. The expedition was led by a man whose name is immortalized in the waters he sailed: Vitus Bering. The bold Dane set off in 1728 intent upon verifying the fishermen's tales. All that he found, however, was that the Bering Sea was very susceptible to fogs. In the end, the sea mists forced him to turn back before he reached American shores.

Thirteen years later Bering set out again into the cold waters. This time he was luckier and the fogs stayed away. The first sight he had of Alaska was the 18,000-foot-high peak of Mount Saint Elias. Bering's men landed on the strange coast, captured a few sea otters and then returned to Russia. The quality of the furs sparked off interest and a prosperous fur trade was soon established. By 1784 there was a permanent Russian settlement, at Three Saints Bay, working the valuable fur trade. But the Russians were neither efficient nor sympathetic rulers. The fur animals were hunted relentlessly and the Russians' treatment of the natives was little better. In 1802 the locals had had enough of their foreign Governor, one Alexander Baranov, and they rose in revolt. They stormed the Russian capital of Sitka and massacred every European, bar one who somehow managed to escape.

Alaska was simply too far from St. Petersburg for the Tsar to be able to rule it effectively. In the 1820s the Russian monarch was forced to open the area up to American and British trappers. Forty years later the fur animals were all but extinct and Alaska was becoming an expensive property for the Tsar. In 1856 Russia suffered defeat at the hands of the British and the French in the Crimean War and the great empire was short of troops, ships and money and by the 1860s Russia was looking for a buyer for Alaska. In 1867 the Russians approached the United States. Secretary of State William Seward was certainly interested and persuaded Congress to part with over $7 million for the territory. In 1868 Alaska formally became part of the United States.

At that time little was known of the region except that it was very large indeed. The very name Alaska told Americans that. The name was derived from the native Aleut word *Alashka*, which means simply, "The Great Land". It was so large that the seven million dollars worked out at just two cents an acre. Size isn't everything and the vast area of what was then considered to be waste land was soon dubbed Seward's Icebox. The purchase was not at all popular with the American people, who felt that the Russians had made them pay a high price for a useless piece of real estate. They could not know that Alaska would turn out to be one of the most wonderful areas of America and to be far more valuable that the price that Seward had paid for his "icebox".

Alaska sprawls across 586,400 square miles of North America, which makes it the largest peninsula in the Western Hemisphere, and could easily be considered as a subcontinent in its own right. The fur-rich coasts which first brought men to the northern land have not been accurately measured, but with all the islands and indents, they are thought to measure some 34,000 miles in extent. The interior is greatly diversified and remarkably beautiful. It includes the tallest mountain in America, which is just a tiny part of immense ranges that march across the state. In the far north, tundra stretches for seemingly-endless distances across the landscape. Further south the coniferous forests spread like a green carpet across almost unimaginably large areas. Yet amid the cold and the permafrost there are areas where the land is fertile and the climate is temperate enough to allow the growing of crops. In fact, the land around Anchorage is some of the best in America for the production of oats, rye, barley and many types of vegetables.

The most immediately striking feature of Alaska is its huge mountain system. It was a mountain that Bering saw when he approached the unknown shores from the west and mountains which continue to dominate the landscape even today. Perhaps the most impressive of all the mountains in Alaska is the tallest peak in the United States and the center of a National Park. Mount McKinley rises from a valley floor which is 1,000 feet above sea level in a dramatic sweep to its pinnacle at over 20,000 feet. The spectacular scene is one of the most impressive in the entire state and it is unfortunate that there is usually so much fog and rain about that it rarely be seen. The only reliable way to see the peak is to go up in an airplane.

The colossal bulk of Mount McKinley is part of a mountain chain which reaches out into the sea as the submarine range of the Aluetians and southwards to form the Cascades of the Pacific Northwest. At Mount McKinley the mountain belt forms a stretch of land sixty miles wide, but at Mount Spurr they spread across 120 miles of the Alaskan landscape. The southern mountains have been formed by the same basic cause as the San Andreas Fault which has often brought devastation to California. The surface of the earth is made up of huge blocks of rock, known as tectonic plates, which fit together like a jigsaw. Unlike a jigsaw, however, the tectonic plates are moving. The huge plate that underlies the Pacific Ocean is moving northwestward in relation to that which forms the North American continent. In California the two plates rub against each other as they slide in opposite directions. If there is the slightest jerk in the movement a major earthquake would result and might devastate whole cities. In Alaska the two plates do not merely slide past each other, they collide.

When the Pacific Plate runs straight into the North American Plate in the Gulf of Alaska it noses down into the depths of the earth. The titanic forces involved have buckled the edge of the American Plate and forced up towering mountains. Folded sedimentary rocks form much of the southern Alaskan mountains, but the collision of the plates had another effect on the geology of the region. As the millions of tons of rock nose-dived down into the earth it melted. Great pressure built up deep below the surface of the earth and enormous quantities of molten rock tried desperately to find a way out to relieve the pressure. In places the molten rock forced its way between layers of sedimentary rocks or up through fissures in the ground. Buried beneath the mountains of southern Alaska are enormous blocks of intruded granite and mineral-rich rocks. The vast masses of liquid, turbulent rock had another effect on the mountains. In some places the hot magma wells to the surface and forms powerful volcanoes, similar to those of the Cascades. There are literally dozens of volcanoes around the coast of Alaska, and nearly fifty of them are active. The symmetrical cones of Shishaldin and Pavlof are both graceful and beautiful, rivalling Mount Kilimanjaro for dramatic quality. Other manifestations of the volcanic forces are more staggering, but rather less beautiful.

On June 6, 1912 the Novarupta Volcano, in the extreme southwest of the state, erupted. The eruption was not one of the sedate, lava emitting affairs characteristic of the Hawaiian Islands, but a cataclysmic blast which had more in common with the eruption of Mount St. Helens. Something in the area of seven cubic miles of rock were thrown into the air. The town of Kodiak suddenly found itself buried beneath a foot-deep layer of ash and pumice which brought it to a virtual standstill. The citizens of Kodiak may have considered themselves lucky as the valley just below the volcano, which had been green and verdant, was filled to a depth of 700 feet by volcanic debris. The dramatic effects did not stop with the direct blast of the eruption. Nobody realized that the towering Mount Katmai was just a shell of rock surrounding a core of molten magma. The eruption of Novarupta opened up new subterranean channels which drained the liquid rock from the center of Katmai. With nothing to support it, the crest of Mount Katmai collapsed in on itself, leaving a yawning chasm where a pinnacle had once been.

Today, the site of the devastating eruption is one of the tourist attractions of the state, included as it is in the borders of Katmai National Monument. The open top of Mount Katmai itself is filled by a beautiful, green lake. The debris-strewn valley is now a maze of intricate channels and deep canyons as the mountain streams cut away at the soft ash and rubble. Underground water is superheated by the hot rock and escapes through vents, earning the area the name of The Valley of the Ten Thousand Smokes.

By contrast with the turbulent, volcanic story of the southern mountains, the ranges in the north, beyond the Arctic Circle, are folded mountains which can be seen as a simple extension of the Rockies. Between the Brooks Range in the north and the volcanic peaks of the south is a region of comparatively low land which is drained by the mighty Yukon River. The mountains are not just taken up by dramatic peaks and snow-covered land; the Alaskan mountains, as nowhere else in America, are the province of the glaciers. In the cold northern land the conditions that prevailed across most of the continent during the Ice Ages are still to be found. Glaciers are massive, slow moving rivers of ice which grind inexorably down the mountains. The glaciers generally originate high up in the mountains where snowfall never melts, even in summer. As the depth of snow increases, the lower levels become compacted into ice. Eventually the weight of ice and snow is so great that the mountain slope can no longer support it and the whole frozen mass begins to move.

Glaciers may move at speeds as low as a few inches a year, but their power is undeniable. The great weight of so much frozen water pushing against the rock is enough to wear it away, but a glacier also picks up bits of stone which act like a giant sandpaper on the rocks. Grinding glaciers enlarge and deepen the valleys they flow through, dumping the rock debris at their end. Where the slope suddenly steepens, an ice fall will result. As the solid ice tries to flow downward, great cracks open up in the glacier surface, creating the crevasses which are such a danger to climbers. Glaciers are a feature of Alaska and occur in great numbers. At one bay, aptly named Glacier Bay, no less than fifteen glaciers reach down out of the mountains to the sea.

In the far north another phenomenon peculiar to Alaska, of all the states, is to be found: permafrost. Permafrost occurs only in extreme conditions of cold, where the ground temperature never has a chance to rise much above freezing. Year-round, the ground remains frozen solid. Any water which might be caught in the soil is trapped there and cannot be used by the plants that would otherwise grow on the land. In some places the surface inches of soil may melt for a few weeks, or even months, in the year and small lichens and grasses have a chance of survival, but the underlying subsoil is always in the grip of winter and no larger plants can survive. A curious feature of permafrost is the formation of pingoes. A pingo is a large block of ice which forms beneath the soil, and as it increases in size it pushes the ground up into a mound. Over the years it continues to grow in size until it has formed a small hill, complete with grass cover. Pingos only survive where their covering of soil and lichens remains intact. As soon as that is broken, the warm sun begins to melt the ice and the hill will soon subside back to its normal, flat state.

It may be thought that in such a hostile environment wildlife would be almost entirely absent. Nothing could be further from the truth. Alaska is the last outpost of the great game animals that once held sway over almost the entire continent. Millions of buffalo once roamed the Great Plains and grazed on the native grasses of the region. By 1900 the sixty million buffalo had been reduced to a mere handful. Relentless hunting destroyed the great herds and farming of the grasslands precluded any possibility of a major comeback. Grizzlies were driven from their native plains and forest so that today they only just manage to survive in the conterminous United States at all.

By contrast, the mighty herds of caribou continue to roam the Alaskan lands as if man had never visited the region. They have never suffered the hunting that destroyed the herds of buffalo, so that the whole fauna that depends on the great herds has survived intact. Caribou are large, even-toed ungulates, very closely related to the reindeer, and are among the largest animals in Alaska. The poorness of the vegetation in the bleak land of Alaska does have a decisive effect on the caribou herds. There are 13 recognized great herds, from the Alaska Peninsula Herd in the extreme southeast to the Porcupine Herd in the northwest, whose range extends deep into Canada. The shifting seasons open up the higher slopes and latitudes to grazing and then close them again. In summer the massive Porcupine Herd wanders northwestward as the retreating snows reveal the lichens of the tundra. As winter closes in they move back again to the winter feeding grounds. The herd travels along set routes that have not varied for centuries and their movements can be predicted accurately.

The 600,000 caribou not only eat the poorest lichens and most succulent willow shoots of the Arctic, they also provide an important link in the food chain of the region. At the lower end of the scale, the millions of mosquitos and warble flies that come out in the summer live upon the blood that they can suck from the caribou. It is not an unusual sight to see groups of caribou retreat to the snowfields in the height of summer to escape from the bites of the winged parasites. More noticeably, the caribou provide food for the packs of wolves which follow them on their seasonal migrations. Caribou are among the few large mammals which can successfully live on such poor grazing as northern Alaska has to offer and are, therefore, perhaps the most important animals in the Alaskan fauna.

Caribou do not take their name from Alaska itself, that accolade goes to a much more powerful animal: the Kodiak bear. On their hind legs, Kodiak bears can easily stand twice as tall as a man and weigh up to 1,800 pounds. They are the largest land carnivores in the world. The Kodiak bear, in common with other Alaskan bears, is really a subspecies of the mighty grizzly which has been pushed to the verge of extinction in the conterminous United States. The enormously powerful animals feed on almost anything that comes within range, including grass when there is nothing else, and are surprisingly agile. Even the largest Kodiak can outrun a man, so it is hardly surprising that they are considered to be perhaps the most dangerous animals in Alaska. Certainly, visitors to national parks are warned against the bears.

One animal which was hunted to extinction in Alaska in the nineteenth century was the huge, shaggy musk ox. The massive beasts are leftovers from the Ice Ages, which have fared somewhat better than the woolly mammoth or woolly rhinoceros. They weigh up to a thousand pounds and are able to live off the sparse lichens and mosses of the far north. When threatened, musk oxen form a circle with the young in the center and the adults facing the outside, with heads lowered. Such a defence mechanism is ideal against wolves, but make the oxen sitting targets for men. After their final annihilation by man in Alaska, a small herd was imported from Greenland and is now thriving on Nunivak Island.

In the rivers of the northernmost state swims a fish which was one of the first reasons for white settlers to come to Alaska and, unlike the sea otter, is still plentiful in the flowing waters of Alaska: the salmon. Just ten years after buying the vast land of Alaska the Americans had opened up a salmon cannery. Before long, the Alaskan salmon industry was the largest in the world and gourmets everywhere thrilled to the taste of salmon caught in the cold, northern land. Other fish soon began to be caught, especially halibut which may reach 300 pounds in weight. Shrimp and crabs are also valuable catches for the tough men who put out from Alsakan ports.

Fishing, as a whole, is the state's second most important industry. It is surpassed by only one other natural resource, that of oil. Now a multi-million dollar industry, it was not oil, however, which was the first mineral to bring men north. That was a mineral with far more popular appeal, a mineral whose lure has never diminished with the centuries: gold. The first strike was made when the land was under the control of the Russians, in 1861, but the fields around Stikine were not particularly rich. Another small strike followed at Juneau in 1880, but it was the massive goldrush to the Klondike in the 1890s that really put Alaska on the map. Thousands of fortune hunters passed through Alaska on their way to the Canadian goldfields, enduring immense hardship on the way. At the Chilkoot Pass, north of Skagway, miners had to climb 1,200 steps cut into the ice in order to ascend the 32-degree slope to the head of the pass. In 1898 the goldrush came to Alaska itself when 20,000 hopefuls descended on Nome. The gold was literally lying on the beaches and the coast was lined with miners' tents for miles. Five years later the interior town of Fairbanks mushroomed as a fresh goldrush centered on the town.

Fairbanks is now experiencing something of a new rush, though this time it is big business and not individual hopefuls that is pouring in. As early as the 1940s geologists had been speculating on the possibility of oilfields north of the Brooks Range. In 1968 the money spent on research finally paid off when Atlantic Richfield and British Petroleum struck oil at Prudhoe Bay. The amount of oil and gas in the field was phenomenal. There are thought to be about 9.5 billion barrels of oil and 26 trillion cubic feet of gas available for exploitation beneath the tundra. South of Atqasuk is another field of about five billion barrels of oil, but it is under the Beaufort Sea that the biggest fields of all are thought to exist. Though they will be hazardous and expensive to drill, the reserves beneath the ocean are expected to top 17 billion barrels of oil and 72 trillion cubic feet of gas.

The oil business has, however, been beset with the same basic problem which has struck at any other business in Alaska. Alaska is so big and so distant from the other states that it is incredibly difficult and costly to transport anything. Luckily oil is a liquid and so the idea of a giant pipeline was born. Completed in 1977, the pipe runs from Prudhoe Bay right across the state to Valdez and cost $9 billion to install. Across a land so naturally diverse and temperamental as Alaska this involved major problems. The pipe had to be insulated, partly to stop the oil from freezing and partly to prevent melting the permafrost. It had to be raised on stilts, or buried beneath the ground, so as not to block the migration routes of the caribou and the wolves. The pipeline also had to be able to withstand earthquakes; after all, in 1964 the most powerful earthquake ever to hit America struck at Prince William Sound.

The natural power and splendor of Alaska remains undiminished and is still able to hold up the progress of man. Even so, the state remains a land of hope and deams for some. As recently as 1967 a group of traditionalist Orthodox Christians came to the state and established a town on the Kenai Peninsula to escape what they saw as the evil influences of the modern United States.

MOUNTAINS

The roof of any nation is its mountains. Soaring into the sky, the rocky pinnacles provide some of the most spectacular scenery and uplifting experiences that a continent has to offer. The United States is endowed with mountains which are among the most beautiful in the world. The Rockies soar up with their ice-encrusted peaks, while the volcanic Cascades smolder threateningly above the West Coast. The whole Western Cordillera, from Canada to Mexico, is a rugged panorama of beauty and spectacular magnificence. But these mountains are relative newcomers to the North American continent, only tracing the story back a "mere" seventy million years. It is the less spectacular, but perhaps more beautiful, mountains of the East which can lay claim to the title of the oldest peaks in America; indeed, they are amongst the oldest mountains in the world.

The story of the Appalachians dates back an almost inconceivably long time, to a period in the history of the earth when not a single creature crawled upon the land and not a single plant soaked up the rays of the sun. More than a billion years ago great masses of liquid rock welled up from deep within the planet and solidified at a depth of many miles from the surface. Almost as soon as they had cooled, these ancient granites began to be uplifted. The vast layers of rock above them were slowly worn away until, three hundred million years after they had been formed, the granite broke through to the surface. Over the next 400 million years the rocks were bent, cracked, eroded and at times flooded by the sea. Fresh strata of sedimentary rocks were layered on top of them and volcanic rocks flowed out from the earth. 300 million years ago, the basement granite was overlaid by some 30,000 feet of sedimentary and volcanic rocks. It was at this time that the specific earth movements which were to lead to the rise of the Appalachians began.

The surface of the earth is not a solid crust. Instead it is made up of several large plates of rock which float on the underlying, fluid mantle, and the subsurface mantle is slowly moving, at the rate of perhaps 3 or 4 inches a year. Quite why it moves is still obscure, but it moves with an irresistible force. As it shifts and surges it jostles the overlying plates of rock. In turn these slowly move around the earth, unleashing titanic forces as they do so. The Pacific Plate is thought to be moving northwestward at the rate of three inches a year. This movement causes the devastating earthquakes which can strike in California and Alaska. Three hundred million years ago similar earth movements began to push into the North American continent from the southeast. The immense force of the shifting tectonic plates was not to be denied and the edge of the continent began to buckle and twist under the pressure. In places the rock split open along cracks hundreds of miles in length. The rock on either side of the faults was forced either up or down. It is the massive rock movements along the lines of these faults which have caused the parallel ridges and valleys so characteristic of the Appalachian Mountains. The mountains continued to rise and twist for over a hundred million years. When they reached their greatest height they were probably as tall, if not taller, than the Rockies are today.

Two hundred million years ago the mountain building stopped. There was no longer a great force ramming into North America from the southeast. Just as nobody is quite sure what started the geological upheaval, no one is really certain why it stopped. But scientists can be confident about what happened next. The irresistible forces of nature got to work and began to wear away the mountain peaks. Erosion can come in many guises, but by far the most efficient and dramatic is water. Falling rain picks up carbon dioxide from the air and becomes a mild acid. This can chemically destroy some of the weaker rocks. More noticeable are the effects of running water. A river, or even a stream, picks up sand and stone on its journey and will tumble them down its course. The tumbling stones and sand act upon the rock as sandpaper acts upon wood, slowly scraping away at the riverbed dislodging other stones, enlarging weaknesses and cutting a channel through the solid rock. Nearly all the river valleys and gorges of the world have been gouged out of the earth by the relentless pounding delivered by gravel and pebbles in the rivers. The Appalachians demonstrate the sheer power of river erosion quite clearly. When the titanic forces of tectonic shifting began to raise the mountains there was already a well-established drainage system. North of Virginia the rivers flowed eastward into the Atlantic, south of Virginia they flowed westward into a vast inland sea which then covered the Great Plains. Despite the great forces which were at work pushing the rocks into the air, the rivers were a match for them. The running waters continued to follow their same old course as before and as fast as the mountains pushed up, the rivers cut channels and gorges through them. To this day, the northern rivers flow eastward and the southern rivers westward, though they had to do a lot of erosional cutting to maintain their courses. It is to the power of the ancient rivers that we owe the existence of the dramatic gorges and river gaps that are such a feature of the Appalachians. At other times freezing can erode mountains. Water can seep into a crack in the rock and when winter comes and the water freezes it expands, splitting a sliver of rock from the hillside. Plants also play their part, breaking the bare rock down into soil which can be more easily removed.

There was one final, and devastating, eroding agent to strike at the Appalachians before they reached the present day: the harshness of the Ice Ages. After standing serene and proud for hundreds of millions of years, the Appalachians were ground and pulverized in just the last two million years. During the Ice Ages the climate of North America became devastatingly colder. Arctic conditions prevailed throughout the Appalachians and reindeer, musk-oxen and hairy mastodons roamed the slopes and valleys. In the northern reaches of the Appalachians mighty glaciers pushed down from the mountaintops and from the north. A glacier is simply a moving river of solid ice. Its solidity and immense depth gives it far more destructive power than a river could ever hope to wield. The grinding weight of ice strips the soil from the rocks and then proceeds to grind the base rocks into dust. At the ends and edges of glaciers the rock debris and dust is dumped in great piles. Glaciers which join another do not cut their beds down to a common level, they remain high above the bed of the main glacier; only their upper levels are balanced.

Any area that has been glaciated has an unmistakable landscape. The valleys are deep and shaped like a U, the steep sides giving way to near level floors. The side glaciers are gone and replaced by streams which tumble in waterfalls to the floor of the main valley. The vast mounds of dumped debris can appear in a variety of guises. Sometimes they form lines of low hills or ridges. Cape Cod is really a glacial deposit which rises above the sea floor just enough to break the ocean surface. More often a moraine, as such deposits are called, will block off part of a valley and trap a lake. Many of the lakes in glaciated regions have been formed by moraines. All these natural forces, uplift and erosion, have gone into the shaping of the oldest mountain chain in the United States.

The mountains themselves can conveniently be divided into two broad geological sections: Old Appalachia and New Appalachia. The terms do not refer to the age of the mountains, for they were all raised at more or less the same time, but to the age of the rocks which form them. Old Appalachia consists mainly of the ancient granites that were formed deep beneath the earth a billion years ago. This system is centered in the north, in Canada and New England, but it pushes its fingers down the eastern side of the mountains to the southern end of the Blue Ridge. New Appalachia was built from the sedimentary rocks which formed over the granites between 700 and 300 million years ago. The new system is basically found in the west, in the Great Valley, the Valley Ridges and the Alleghenies.

The different types of rock found in the two systems, the old and the new, have quite different properties. In the erosion which has taken place over the millennia, the granites have formed quite different structures from the shales and limestones of New Appalachia. The basic properties of the underlying rocks have had a drastic effect upon the scenery and vegetation that we see today.

The White Mountains of New Hampshire are made up of tough, resistant rock which was glaciated several times in the past two million years. This scenically beautiful region, little more than 50 miles in diameter, has long been the favorite vacation spot for New England. It is Yankee country through and through, the heritage of the early days managing to peep through the more modern, tourist-oriented towns and resorts. Far older than the Yankees are the mountains themselves. Sliced through the western parts of the mountains is Franconia Notch, now a state park. High above the valley rises the gaunt visage of the Old Man of the Mountains. A curious rock formation wrought by the hand of nature, the rock outcrop bears a striking resemblance to a man's profile. In the depths of the valley runs the Flume, an 800-foot long chasm with sheer, seventy-foot tall walls. The babbling brook which runs through the Flume gives it a calmness and serenity all its own, while the light filtering down from above divorces it from the real world. Nearby is the well-known Lost River. The narrow gorge, known as Kinsman Notch, is a jumble of huge boulders left behind by the glaciers and of natural caves tunnelled by running water. The small river which flows through the notch continually disappears behind massive rocks or into tunnels on its journey through the valley. Towering above all in the White Mountains is Mount Washington, which at 6,288 feet is nearly the tallest peak in the Appalachians.

South of the White Mountains, the domination of the limestones and shales becomes apparent in the New Appalachia regions. The craggy peaks and outcrops of bare rock so characteristic of Old Appalachia are gone, but the limestone hills of Virginia have sights far more wonderful than the Old Man of the Mountains to offer. The wonders of the Virginia hills are not immediately apparent to the eye and in many cases were not found until quite recently. They are caves. Limestone is one of the rocks susceptible to attack by the weak carbonic acid found in rainwater. As the water seeps down into the ground it discovers the weak spots in the rocks. It creeps into the cracks formed during the uplifting of the mountains, all the time dissolving the very rock itself. Over thousands of years the slow trickle of water will hollow out caves and caverns deep beneath the earth. The water may form subterranean rivers which wear away the rock even more quickly. It is the chemical erosion of limestone which forms the great caverns for which the Virginia hills are so famous.

Rainwater does not only have a destructive effect upon the limestone, but it can also create formations of stone, and it is this which has made the caves so popular with the public. As water seeps through the rock it picks up mineral solids which would normally remain dissolved and be washed away. Where a trickle of water comes out into a large cavern it is subject to evaporation. As the water hangs on the cave roof some of it evaporates, leaving its load of minerals behind. The gradual build up of water-deposited minerals results in stalactites, stalagmites and all the other wonderfully beautiful cave formations. Great curtains of stone seem to hang from the ceilings and pillars rise up from the floors. The limestone hills around Front Royal, Salem and the Shenandoah may be less visually attractive than the gaunt granites of Old Appalachia, but they have some remarkable hidden treasures.

The Appalachians are by far the oldest mountains in the United States and they were the first to be explored and mapped by white men. Far to the west, however, rose a range of mountains larger in both height and extent than the eastern mountains. The mighty Western Cordillera had been glimpsed from ships sailing along what are now the Californian, Oregon and Washington coasts, and Spanish missionaries in the San Joaquin Valley had penetrated the foothills, but in the year 1800 the mountains were otherwise unknown. On the maps of the period the whole region is left blank, or filled in with imaginary rivers and valleys. It was into this unknown and possibly dangerous land that Lewis and Clark ventured in the first years of the last century. They crossed over the Rockies, from what is now Montana to Idaho. They were simply stunned by the natural beauty that they found: soaring pinnacles of rock and sweeping snowfields met their eyes in unparalleled splendor. The Easterners had never seen anything as remarkable as the ice-encrusted mountains and the tree-filled valleys of the Rockies. In less than two hundred years the mighty Rockies have gone from a blank space on the map to being almost the richest mineral fields in the United States.

The mountains themselves are, of course, far older than the history of civilization in the area. The two centuries of white settlement are as nothing to the age of the Rockies. The first large earth movements swept the area during the days when the dinosaurs still walked the land, about 150 million years ago, during the Jurassic period. The area had until then lain beneath the sea and massive beds of sedimentary rocks had formed. These were slowly raised, though as with the raising of the Appalachians nobody is quite sure why, and formed a large upland. The earth movements did not stop there. The mountains of western Wyoming and adjacent areas were formed by a process known as thrust sheeting. Great sheets of rock, several thousand feet thick and as much as 150 miles long, have been lifted up and driven along the ground for as much as 30 miles. They now lie on top of rocks older than themselves and testify to the frightening power of the tectonic plates. Further south, in Utah and Nevada, great cracks opened up in the earth and vast blocks of land rose or fell thousands of feet as the earth's crust continued to buckle. The Eastern mountains, which rise from the Great Plains in such a dramatic manner, are the result of numerous vertical uplifts. Some, such as the Colorado Front Range, are vast, but most are about 800 square miles in extent. It is the uneven weathering of rocks within the uplifts which has created the spectacular peaks and valleys of the area.

Not all the Western Cordillera is classified by geologists as the Rockies. The mighty Sierra Nevada, for example, seems to have been built up at about the same time as the earliest activity of the Rockies but as the result of quite different pressures. About 100 million years ago the mountain building slowed down and finally stopped, leaving the Sierra Nevada at the mercy of the erosion agents that had already been working on the Appalachians for millions of years. The Cascades also have little to do with the forces that raised the Rockies. The mighty range, which lies about a hundred miles inland throughout the northwestern conterminous United States, is almost certainly volcanic in origin. All the larger peaks, including Mounts

Hood and Rainier, are extinct volcanoes which reached their present size by spewing forth lava and ash. The 10,457-foot tall Mount Lassen is still considered to be active, although its last splutterings were nearly seventy years ago. One peak which nobody can doubt is still active lies in the far northern reaches of the Cascades. On May 18, 1980 Mount St. Helens exploded with a force 500 times that of the Hiroshima bomb. One and a half cubic miles of rock was pulverized and flung into the air. Dozens of people were killed and many more had lucky escapes. A hundred and fifty square miles of forest was flattened and turned into a desolate, gray landscape.

Another feature of the Western Cordillera that everybody has taken as fact for well over a century is that it is immensely rich in minerals. Many years ago, at a place called Sutter's Mill, a man found a nugget of gold in the stream and the rush was on. Thousands of hopeful miners poured into the area armed with backpacks and shovels. Some found their dream of riches, but far more made only small strikes and were then robbed of even that by professional gamblers and unscrupulous store owners. The great gold rushes which rocked the American West at intervals throughout the pioneer days were the most famous mineral strikes in the region. The combination of easy wealth and lawlessness have made the gold towns irresistible to story writers and film makers for generations. Less dramatic than the wild days of the gold rushes are the later and far more important finds of less romantic minerals.

Throughout Montana, Utah and Arizona are vast fields of copper which produce almost all that mined in the United States. Further north, the iron ore fields of Wyoming and Utah support heavy industry in the immediate vicinity. Also topping the list of minerals found in the mountains are the more recently useful deposits of uranium, molybdenum and beryllium. The only mineral that today excites the imagination as much as gold is oil. Oil is a strange mineral. It does not stay in the rocks in which it is formed like metal ore does. It is able to seep through permeable rocks, such as sandstone, and generally moves upward. Left to itself, any substantial body of oil would seep up until it reached the surface and then run away leaving civilization without the internal combustion engine, and a great deal besides. Fortunately for man, oil cannot move through impermeable rocks and can thus become trapped. The eastern Rockies make ideal ground for oilfields, where the block faulting of the region has cut off many huge sections of oil-bearing rock from other permeable layers. Surrounded by impermeable rocks, the oil has remained in position for million of years until the drilling of man provided an escape route. Wyoming, Montana, Colorado, New Mexico and Utah are the major oil producers in the Rockies. The western section of the mountains has little oil for the simple reason that the peaks were formed by folding, not faulting. In nearly all cases a folded band of rock reaches the surface somewhere, or meets another band of permeable rock. Any oil that may have existed in the western Rockies has long since crept away and been lost to man.

In the Unita Mountains of Wyoming and Colorado, oil is found in a form that does not seep away. The shales of the area hold a solid hydrocarbon which, when specially treated, produces liquid oil. The amount of oil tied up in the shales is astronomical, making even the experts gasp. Unfortunately, the cost of the treatment is also vast and simple economics make it unprofitable to extract the oil. When other fields run out, however, the United States will still have huge reserves to call upon, even if the cost will be rather high.

The first men to visit the great Western Cordillera, men like Jim Bridger and Jedediah Smith, were not immediately struck by the richness of the mineral fields, and even today it is not the most apparent thing about the Rockies. The feature which hits the modern visitor, just as it hit the earliest mountain men, is the immense beauty of the mountains. When Jim Bridger came down from the mountains claiming to have found a mountain of glass and a river which cooked fish and springs that shot boiling water a hundred feet into the air, nobody believed him. They did not listen to John Colter either. Even in 1869 stories from the Yellowstone were dismissed. It was not until William Henry Jackson hauled a bulky camera into the mountains in 1871 and actually photographed the natural wonders that the tales were believed. Copies of the photographs were presented to every Senator and Representative in Washington. In 1872 Yellowstone became the first National Park in the world.

Since that time it has not only been geothermal areas that have merited National Park status. Vast tracts of mountain have been put aside for the enjoyment and pleasure of the country's millions. It is no longer necessary to trek for miles, with a burro as your only companion, to see the wild and natural beauty of the mountains. Their splendor and magnificence have been put aside to be preserved for all time.

As the roof for the continent, the peaks of the Appalachians and Rockies are magnificent. The majesty of their scenery is the result of millions upon millions of years of titanic upheavals and shifting rocks. The mountains form surely the most magnificent and powerful images on the continent, belittling man's efforts if only by their very size.

LAKES

Looking at a map, lakes are perhaps the most noticeable feature of the United States. The vast blue areas of the Great Lakes seem to hang over the northeastern corner of the continent like a chain of sapphires. Across the northern plains stretch a sprinkling of tiny jewels, each an integral part of the prairies and each owing its existence to the geology of the area. In the west the myriad lakes nestled beneath the peaks of the Western Cordillera interrupt the jagged peaks and ridges with a network of blue.

Yet lakes are surprisingly unimportant in the natural workings of the earth's water supply. The world's lakes hold less than one half of one percent of continental fresh water, a staggeringly small amount for such prominent features. The rest of the precious liquid is held by streams, rivers, glaciers and, most important of all, in ground water. Ground water is the term used to describe any water which is held in rocks, underground water systems, or simply in the soil. Despite containing such a low amount of the total fresh water, it is known that lakes account for 98 percent of the fresh water available for use by man. In a modern industrial society fresh water plays an increasingly important role. It is used by people for drinking, washing and for a variety of sanitary purposes; it is used by industry for cooling, for chemical reactions and to dilute noxious wastes and it is used by agriculture for irrigation of crops in dry seasons or arid areas. The United States is currently using over 22 billion gallons a day for domestic purposes 141 billion gallons for irrigation and a staggering 160 billion gallons per day for industry. These massive demands cannot be met by water networks which rely on rivers, which may be seasonal or unreliable. They need to draw on a steady and constant supply, and that means lakes.

With such large demands placed upon the nation's lakes, it is comforting to realize that the United States includes some of the largest lakes in existence and a fair proportion of the earth's lake waters. The Great Lakes, the most noticeable and prominent of all American lakes, are truly great. Lake Superior contains some 3,000 cubic miles of water, which makes it the third largest body of fresh water in the world. Taken as a whole the Great Lakes system holds a steady 6,000 cubic miles of fresh water. This total places the system above the largest single lake, Russia's Lake Baikal, in the table of capacities. Indeed, the Great Lakes hold close on a fifth of all the lake water in the world. When this is added to the total of other United States' lakes, a capacity of over a quarter of the world's total is reached; a truly amazing total for a single nation.

Lakes can develop for a variety of reasons, some of them definitely more dramatic and spectacular than others, but the Great Lakes were formed by ice. Eighteen thousand years ago massive glaciers crunched their way across the United States. The frozen rivers were thousands of feet thick and weighed billions of tons. The power of the slow-moving ice floes was tremendous. They were so heavy and the force driving them so irresistible that they gouged out great valleys in the living rock and scraped away any vestige of soil. Their great weight forced some areas literally to sink as the rocks bowed beneath the crushing weight. All this was to have a profound effect on the area around the Great Lakes.

Before the advance of the great ice sheets a complex and comprehensive drainage system of streams and rivers existed in the area, but this was radically altered by the glaciers. Some valleys were deepened by the crunching ice as it gouged lumps out of the rock. Other areas were blocked by great mounds of sand and gravel debris dumped by the glaciers. Such piles of debris are known as moraines and are significant features of the environment in many parts of the world. As the powerful ice retreated to the north, their effects began to be seen. At first the lakes which formed in the gouged basins of Lakes Michigan and Erie flowed southward into the Mississippi. They did this because the glaciers were just to the north and blocked any other route. The ice continued to melt and to retreat so that before long the whole of the Great Lakes region was free of its terrible grip. At one point, when the glaciers still blocked drainage to the north, Lakes Superior, Huron and Michigan joined to form one single, massive lake, known to modern scientists as Lake Algonquin. When the ice pulled back from the northern shores of the lakes it exposed the lowlands to the east of Georgian Bay. The waters of the lakes gushed across the area and down the Ottawa Valley. The low-lying land, however, had been forced down by the weight of the ice sheets which once covered it. When the glaciers had gone it began to rise. Shortly, in geological terms, after the drainage down the Ottawa had begun, it stopped. The retreat of the glaciers had opened up the route and had just as surely closed it again. The waters of the upper lakes were forced to find another outlet. They found it through the lower lakes. By three thousand years ago the present-day layout of the Great Lakes had been established.

For many centuries the Great Lakes were the haunts of the Indians. They paddled their birchbark canoes upon the still, and not so still, waters. They fished the depths, hunted along the shores and waged terrible wars upon each other for possession of the best fishing or hunting grounds. It was not until the arrival of the white man that the written history of the Great Lakes began.

In 1535 the Frenchman Jacques Cartier sailed up the St. Lawrence as far as Montreal. There the Indians told him of the great fresh water seas that lay upstream. The upper reaches of the St. Lawrence were, unfortunately, held by hostile Iroquois and further progress was barred. It was not until 1615 that another Frenchman, the intrepid Samuel de Champlain, became the first white man to set eyes upon the Great Lakes, which had long been the subjects of legend. The coming of the white man did not, however, end the bitter fighting of the region. Champlain himself got mixed up in a tribal war and was lucky to escape with his life. Fighting erupted again during the French and Indian War, and during the War of 1812 a major naval engagement was fought on the waters of Lake Erie.

Today, however, peace has at last come to the shores and waters of the Great Lakes, and neither the United States nor Canada maintain fortifications or naval forces in the area. Indeed, the waters, in the shape of the St. Lawrence Seaway, are symbolic of cooperation between the two countries. The lakes had always been important trade routes between Canada and the United States, but mercantile shipping was hampered by the fact that it could not reach the ocean. The few canals which bypassed the rapids and falls between the upper lakes and the sea could only accommodate small barges. Goods had to be laboriously loaded on and off the barges to complete the journey. The seaway cost $446 million dollars to construct and now allows ships up to 730 feet long to steam from the Atlantic to Chicago. Some 14 million tons of grain is exported from the Midwest by way of the Great Lakes. Rather more tonnage of iron ore from Labrador and Quebec is coming up the Seaway to keep the industries of Detroit and Chicago in business. The Great Lakes not only dominate the map and water balance of the northeast, they also contribute greatly to the economic life of the region.

The Great Lakes may hold the bulk of America's lake water, but there are only five of them, while there are literally thousands of other types of lakes, both large and small. One of the strangest form of lake in the United States is the walled variety found chiefly in Iowa. Instead of the lake forming in a hollow of land these lakes are surrounded by mounds, or walls, of earth and stones. Quite why this should be was for many years a mystery and excited much comment. More recently, however, a plausible solution has been put forward. The lakes are invariably on level ground of a particular type and are shallow. In winter the lake freezes solid and the expanding water pushes minute amounts of sand and gravel outwards from the center. From a small beginning, little more than a puddle, an Iowan lake can gradually build up walls and push them outwards until it reaches a fair size.

Lakes can be formed in other, equally bizarre, circumstances. In Washington State, Moses Lake was almost certainly formed when vast quantities of sand were blown by the wind in such a way that when they came to rest they blocked off a basin and trapped waters behind. Far more prevalent than wind-blown debris in the formation of lakes is water-carried matter. The effects of waterborne deposits on the formation of lakes is perhaps best seen along the Mississippi. Once the river winds out into the flat, lower reaches of its course, it meanders and snakes across the landscape. At every turn there is a tendency to cut away the outside of a bend and to deposit sand on the inside. Inevitably, the river course changes, sometimes dramatically. It is not at all unusual to find whole loops of river cut off from the main channel. These loops are, of course, still full of water and form lakes known as oxbows. Such lakes are common in most floodplains, but especially on the Mississippi. The Father of Waters has also created a whole network of lakes and channels in its delta where the slowing waters dump their burden of sediment. Banks and levees are created which can cut off stretches of water or create hollows in which lakes can form.

Far more dramatic than the slow process of deposition and erosion which form river lakes was a cataclysm which struck southwestern Oregon about 6,000 years ago. Mount Mazama exploded with a deafening roar. Clouds of smoke and ash were hurled into the air. Searing waves of burning air swept across the landscape destroying vast areas of the surrounding forest. It was a volcanic outburst far more powerful than that of Mount St. Helens, which hit the headlines in 1980. When the smoke had cleared and the violent explosions ceased, the damage was laid bare. The entire mountain had been ripped apart. Where the peak had once been there was nothing but a yawning chasm. Unlike the more recent Mount St. Helens crater, that of Mount Mazama had no outlet and water began to gather. Today, the whole crater left by the titanic explosion is filled with water. Still there is no outlet, the evaporation of water from the surface matches the inflow from rains and melted snows. The intensely blue lake is 1,932 feet deep and is one of the spectacles of the Northwest. The volcano did not destroy itself in the violent blast, it continued to erupt. More peaceful outpourings of cinder have occurred over the years and Wizard Island in the lake is the result of one such outburst.

An equally spectacular cause of a depression in which a lake may later form is the impact of a meteor crashing to earth. The sheer force of a mass of iron and rock smashing into the ground is enough to create a sizeable crater. Lake Ungava, in Quebec, is a fine example of such a lake, while the bay lakes of southeast America may also have been caused by meteorites.

Most lakes, however, have been formed by rather less spectacular events. The glaciers of the Ice Ages had a profound effect upon the mountains of America. In the Rockies, particularly, lakes formed by glacial action are to be found. Glaciers grind away at the rock over which they travel, picking up all sorts of gravel and debris as they move. This assortment of stones is then dumped by the glaciers at their ends or edges in the form of moraines. Such moraines can easily block off valleys, forming a depression. It is in such basins that many of the mountain lakes have been formed. Other mountain lakes are formed in glacial potholes. Such holes are sheer-sided cylindrical shafts cut by glaciers in the bedrock. Quite how they were formed is still uncertain, but the shafts are ready-made for the collection of water.

A million years ago, a vast lake covered some 20,000 square miles of Utah, Nevada and Idaho. Today that lake has gone, but remnants of it can still be found. Over the years the waters have evaporated, leaving behind all the minerals and salts that were found in the much larger lake. The largest vestige is the Great Salt Lake of northern Utah. Large amounts of water flow into the lake every year, but the heat is such that evaporation more than keeps up with inflow. The result is that any mineral salts brought into the lake stay there when the water disappears. Over the years this has created a body of water which has far higher salinity levels than any other lake, higher indeed than the sea. It is generally around 15 feet deep and rarely reaches more than 35 feet in depth. Being surrounded by flat land the lake can easily spread its shores if it receives extra water. The changing weather around the lake alternately floods and parches the area. In 1876, the Great Salt Lake covered 2,400 square miles but by 1962 it had shrunk to just 950 square miles. The great body of salt water was first reported by the hardy mountain man, Jim Bridger. As with his tales of the Yellowstone country, not many people believed him.

Today, man is adding to the nation's rota of lakes with several fine creations of his own. He has constructed vast dams across mighty rivers, creating great artificial lakes behind them. The dams have been built for a variety of reasons. Some generate electricity, some quench the thirsts of cities, while others bring life-giving irrigation to arid farming regions. In more remote areas, the lakes formed by dams are given over to wildlife and scientific research, but more accessible lakes are the focus of recreational activity, with fishing and yachting high on the list of pastimes. But even on such artificial stretches of water as this the natural environment of America is taking over. Shore plants line the sides of the artificial lakes and fish sport in the waters. The lakes of America are among her most treasured and valuable natural wonders.

The many features of America are staggering in themselves. The mountains, valleys, volcanoes and all the other natural wonders are enough to make men marvel at the work of nature. But taken together, America is far more than the sum of its parts. Nowhere else on earth is the same range of untouched grandeur to be found; nowhere else has nature endowed a land with so rich a legacy of beauty and majesty. With so many natural wonders within its borders, America is a natural wonder in itself.

The natural world is forever changing. At sunset the soft, golden glow of watery sunlight spreads through Ladybird Johnson Grove (facing page), bringing a sense of magic to the air. A few short hours later and the trees will be plunged into a darkness which lends a threatening and foreboding feeling to the place. In time the very trees will collapse, to be replaced by others. Many of these ever-changing scenes have been captured by the National Park Service to be preserved forever. Ladybird Johnson Grove stands in Redwood National Park, California.

CANYONS

The foaming, tumbling waters of America's rivers have created some of the most spectacular scenery in the world. Their powerful currents smash boulders and carry tons of grit along their channels. Over the millenia this pounding has gouged great canyons from the earth. Sheer walls of rock rise to dizzying heights on either side as the Colorado races through the Grand Canyon in Arizona. The massive bastions of stone which rise to heights of 5,300 feet above the Colorado are sedimentary strata dating back millions of years. The cutting action of the waters at Lodore Canyon has revealed ancient rocks of immense interest to scientists. Trapped within these hundred million year old strata are the fossils of massive dinosaurs which once walked the area and are now revealed in the canyon walls. Even older are the brooding rocks of the Black Canyon of the Gunnison which are so old that life itself did not exist when they were created. Not all the gorges of America are the plunging chasms and surging waters of the massive canyons, however. In Utah the winding creeks and seeping rainwater have delicately sculptured the stone into beautiful columns, pinnacles and arches. Canyonlands and Arches National Parks enclose some of the most fantastic rock formations to be found in any country, but it is Bryce Canyon which takes the prize for the greatest concentration of fairytale spires and bridges. Whether they be yawning abysses or delicately wrought formations the canyons of America are a priceless treasure to be cared for and wondered at by all.

(Left) the Grand Canyon, Arizona, seen from Hopi Point on the South Rim.

The red rock areas of the Southwest contain some of the most magnificent canyons in America. (Left) late afternoon near Peekaboo Spring, (far left) Island in the Sky and (bottom right) a view from Island in the Sky, all in Canyonlands National Park, Utah. Elsewhere in Utah can be found North Window (right), Upper Fiery Furnace (below right) and South Window (below far right), while the spectacular Canyon de Chelly (below) lies in Arizona.

Strictly speaking Bryce Canyon (left, far left, and facing page, top left and top right), Utah, is not a canyon at all, as no major river flows through it; the delicate tracery being formed by countless trickles of rainwater. The Virgin River, which rises near Bryce Canyon, cuts its own small chasm (facing page, bottom), near the Sentinel. Double Arch (above), also in Utah, can only be reached by a two-mile footpath. (Overleaf) the sheer scale of the Santa Elena Canyon, Texas, is staggering.

In a small area of southeastern Utah are concentrated perhaps the most fantastic rock formations to be found in any American canyon. Northwest of Monticello

lies the Needles District (center left), drained by Salt Creek, which flows into the Colorado River. The part played by the creek in the sculpting of the rocks along the canyon must take second place to the effects of chemical weathering, rainwater and wind-blown sand. In the hills above the creek stands Squaw Flat (top left). Just forty miles to the northeast, near Moab, stands Delicate Arch (above) and The Devils Garden (bottom left).

(Above) the waters of Wakheena Falls tumble down the side of the Columbia River Gorge. The Gorge forms the border between Oregon and Washington and is an important route through the western mountains. The dry lands of Utah are full of desert blooms and strange rock formations, such as The Organ (left). Looking very much like its namesake, Angel Arch (top right) lies in Canyonlands, while further removed from the original is the Garden of Eden (top center). (Far left) Bryce Canyon. (Top left) rock formations in Montana. (Overleaf) the thousand-foot walls of Pine Creek Canyon, Utah, from Canyon Overlook.

In Dinosaur National Monument, Colorado, the Green River carves the Canyon of Lodore (top right). As the layers of rock are cut away ancient sediments are revealed, displaying the fossilized bones of dinosaurs. (Far right) the Rio Grande near South Fork, Colorado. (Center right) Mule Ear Peak, Texas. (Right) a sign in North Dakota. (Above) Turks head cacti on the Virgin Islands. The Grand Tetons (top left) in Wyoming are riven by dozens of canyons.

Cannon Ball
Concretions

Salt Creek rises in southern Utah and, after carving its canyon (top right), flows into the Colorado, which crosses into Arizona just north of Lee's Ferry (center far right), whence it plunges into the Grand Canyon. Another small stream with a mighty canyon is Oak Creek, which flows past Cathedral Rock (above) just south of Flagstaff, in Arizona. Further north the canyon walls were put to good use by ancient Indians. In Mesa Verde National Park, Colorado,

are the cliff houses (right), whose inhabitants left after severe droughts in the 13th century. (Center right) part of Big Bend National Park in Texas.

(Far right) Canyonlands. Bryce Canyon (remaining pictures) has natural bridges, as at Navajo Loop Trail, turrets and spires.

(Facing page) Bryce Canyon, (top) from Rainbow Point and (bottom) along Navajo Loop. Capitol Gorge (this page), also in Utah, exhibits the many effects of erosion.

(Overleaf) East and West Mittens and Merrick Butte in Monument Valley. This desert area has featured in numerous westerns, particularly those directed by John Ford.

The canyons of the arid Southwest show the finest variety of scale and beauty imaginable. Bryce Canyon, seen (centre left) from Bryce Point, is a marvel of crevices and pinnacles. The canyon takes its name from Ebenezer Bryce, a Scottish Mormon who lived here in the 1870s. The Little Colorado River Gorge, (above) near Gray Mountain in Arizona, has been eroded by a seasonal stream, while the Grand Canyon (facing page) was cut by the continually flowing Colorado. (Left) the brooding Black Canyon of the Gunnison, Colorado.

The Grand Canyon of the Colorado (these pages and overleaf), Arizona, is the largest and most spectacular in the world. (Left) from Moran Point, (bottom) from Hopi Point and (facing page, top and overleaf) from Yaki Point.

Near Sapinero, Colorado, the Gunnison is dammed to form the Blue Mesa Reservoir (left). (Below) an explanatory sign in Texas. (Bottom) Little Missouri, North Dakota. (Facing page: top) Oak Creek Canyon, Arizona; (bottom left) Big Bend, Texas and (bottom right) Bryce Canyon, Utah.

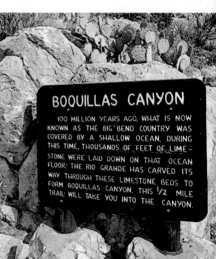

BOQUILLAS CANYON

100 MILLION YEARS AGO, WHAT IS NOW KNOWN AS THE BIG BEND COUNTRY WAS COVERED BY A SHALLOW OCEAN. DURING THIS TIME, THOUSANDS OF FEET OF LIMESTONE WERE LAID DOWN ON THAT OCEAN FLOOR. THE RIO GRANDE HAS CARVED ITS WAY THROUGH THESE LIMESTONE BEDS TO FORM BOQUILLAS CANYON. THIS 1/2 MILE TRAIL WILL TAKE YOU INTO THE CANYON.

The drainage basin of the Colorado River extends over vast areas of the Southwest and eventually dumps its waters into the Gulf of Mexico. It contains some of the most spectacular canyons and rock formations in America, among them South Park Avenue (top) and Zion Canyon, where can be found the Watchman (right), both in Utah, and Lodore Canyon on the Green River in Colorado (left). Further north can be found Roaring Mountain, Wyoming (far right). In California the jagged peaks of the Sierra Nevada plunge precipitously down at Junction Ridge in Kings Canyon (top right), Kings Canyon National Park. (Above) the towering peaks of the Coast Range in Alaska.

FORESTS

Spreading like a rich, green mantle across the continent, the forests of America bring many moods to the landscape. On warm summer days there can be no more serene a place than a New England wood. The insects hum quietly through the leafy greenery and squirrels scamper from branch to branch in search of nuts and seeds. But when the dark clouds gather and lightening flashes from the sky the forests are transformed into writhing worlds where the rushing wind throws the trees into torment and swirls the leaves into the skies. Perhaps the best time to visit these woods is in the fall when the trees turn to gold and russet and the leaves begin to drop. Far to the west, beyond the Great Plains, rise other forests, far removed from the deciduous cover of New England. The woodlands which blanket the lower slopes of the Western Cordilleras are largely made up of conifers which do not shed their leaves in the fall but remain green throughout the year, even when the white hand of winter is laid across the land. On the western slopes of the Californian mountains rise the most majestic of all the timber in America. The giant redwoods with their cinnamon colored bark tower more than three hundred feet into the cool air of the Sierras. It is not only for their scenic grandeur that the forests are valued, they are an important source of timber and wood which is used for a variety of purposes by modern Americans. The forests are not only beautiful to look at, they are an increasingly valuable asset to the nation.

(Left) aspen forest in Colorado.

High in the Californian
Sierras are the largest living
things on earth: the sequoias
(these pages). Growing in
groves (right and center left)
the trees reach huge sizes,
shown by the fallen giants
(bottom pictures). Fire
helps germination but commonly
damages older trees (below).

Tropical Hawaii shelters forest flowers in profusion, there being at least 15,000 species of orchid, some of which are shown (above, above left and top center left), alone. Perhaps the most spectacular bloom is the bird of paradise flower (far left), though the rocket protea (top right), plumeria (top far left) and water lily (left) are just as beautiful. Many flowers, such as those shown (top center right) are used in traditional leis.

Forest cover is highly
dependent upon climatic
conditions. The Smoky
Mountains, (far left) at Le
Conte Creek, are ideal for

deciduous trees. The Great Plains are generally too dry for trees, but the rivers are often lined with timber, as at (center left) the Snake River in Wyoming. The lower slopes of the Rocky Mountains are ideal for aspens which spread like a golden carpet across the hills, (above) at Independence Pass, Colorado. In the Sneffels Range (top left), also in Colorado, the change from aspen to conifer to bare rock as altitude increases can be clearly seen. On the western slopes conifers again proliferate, as (left) at Lassen Peak, California.

The western conifer forests exhibit a wealth of diversity: (below) Tunnel Rock, California; (left) Liberty Bell and (bottom left) Grove of Patriarchs, Washington; (bottom right and facing page, bottom pictures) redwoods, California; (facing page, top) Ladybird Johnson Grove, California and (overleaf) Dream Lake, Colorado.

(Facing page): the exceedingly heavy rains in Northwestern Washington bring rainforest (top) to Olympic National Park; (bottom left) a glory bush blossom from Hawaii and (bottom right) a lady's slipper from Minnessota. (This page): a brook in the Blue Ridge Mountains of Virginia (top left); (top right) Hawaiian candle bush; (far left) Ixora, from Hawaii; (left) Turkshead lily from Virginia and (above) an Hawaiian bloom.

Fall brings a stunning array of color to the forests of America, particularly in Vermont (left) and Colorado; (far left) Crystal Creek and (bottom left) Maroon Creek near Aspen. (Bottom) bare trunks in Yellowstone National Park, Wyoming. (Below) a leafy aster and (bottom center) a golden columbine, both from Utah.

VOLCANIC ACTIVITY

When Mount St. Helens exploded with a deafening roar it sent a burning wind of destruction many miles across Washington State, a cloud of ash across the Northwest and a pall of realization across the nation. The numerous volcanic mountains of the northwest had long been known as scenic wonders. The fact that a solid mountain could simply rip itself to bits and cause such devastation was almost unthinkable. In far off Hawaii, however, such an idea was not so unbelievable. Ever since man first settled on the islands, the mountains have been spewing forth molten lava and sending fiery devastation across the landscape, driving people from their homes. The calderas still simmer, for the pent up forces of nature are still at work in Hawaii. Recent outpourings of lava spread like black ribbons across the green land, while amid black ash fields gaunt trees stand dead in the sunlight. These islands are easily the largest American volcanoes; they have their bases on the ocean floor and rise steadily for thousands of feet until they break the surface and then climb hundreds more into the sky. In Wyoming a gentler side of volcanic activity is revealed. The thermal waters of Yellowstone heave and bubble through underground systems until they rise to the surface in dramatic geysers and beautifully colored pools. The hot waters bring soluble minerals up from deep within the earth and deposit them in the form of terraces and rings. Whatever form it takes, the volcanic activity of America can be a beautiful and awe-inspiring sight.

(Left) Bumpass Hell, Lassen Volcanic National Park, California.

Yellowstone National Park (these pages)
is one of the most consistently
spectacular volcanic sites in America.
Though it lacks the destructive force of

a Mount St. Helens, Yellowstone bubbles and steams as the molten rock churns just below the surface of the vast collapsed caldera of Wyoming.

(Above) sunset lends an appropriate light to Fire-ball River. (Left and center left) algae and bacteria stain the hot waters of Grand Prismatic

Spring, a 370-foot diameter pool. (Top left) the same microscopic life tinges the land around Grotto Geyser a distinctive red.

The Hawaii Islands, created by lava erupting from the ocean floor, are totally volcanic. Lava columns (top center) and volcanic rocks at Waimea Canyon (bottom right) and the Pali Coast (below and facing page, top right) are reminders of this origin. At Halemaumau Firepit (bottom) the fearsome forces are still active.

A recent eruption on Hawaii Island brought death and destruction in its wake. At Devastation Trail (above) a boardwalk takes visitors across a brooding landscape of black pumice and ash and ghostly white trees killed by the eruption. At Yellowstone, volcanically heated water wells to the surface at Grand Prismatic Spring (right) and Percolating Spring (top right), in the West Thumb Geyser Basin. Morning Glory Pool (overleaf) owes its beautiful colors to the algae and bacteria which live at varying depths. As the water rises it cools, allowing the

survival of various species,
each with a distinctive color.
As the water cools and runs
away it is tinged rust red by
the microscopic life.

The steaming Firehole River (far left) of Wyoming is fed by the hot springs of Yellowstone (remaining pictures). (Left) Grand Prismatic Spring, (below) Morning Glory Pool, (below left) Spasm Geyser, (bottom right) Midway Geyser Basin and (bottom left) West Thumb Geyser Basin.

Yellowstone's Minerva Terrace is formed of travertine (left), brought from deep within the earth by the hot waters. Bison are attracted to Yellowstone in the winter as the high ground temperature keeps the snow thin: (far left) in Midway Geyser Basin and (bottom right) in Black Sand Basin. Geysers are the most spectacular features of the park: Daisy Geyser (bottom left) erupts very erratically; Castle Geyser (inset left) may be the oldest in the park and Old Faithful (inset right) is one of the largest. (Overleaf) Opalescent Pool.

Yellowstone reveals the
gentler side of volcanic
activity: (right) Grotto
Geyser; (above) the delicate
Minerva Terrace; (far right)
West Thumb Geyser Basin; (top
far right) Castle Geyser and
(top center and overleaf,
right) Old Faithful. The
destructive force of America's
volcanoes was exemplified by
Mount St. Helens when it
exploded on May 18, 1980,
devastating more than 150
square miles of forest.
(Overleaf, top left) Mount St.
Helens before the eruption and
(overleaf, bottom left) the
destruction caused by the
blast around Spirit Lake.

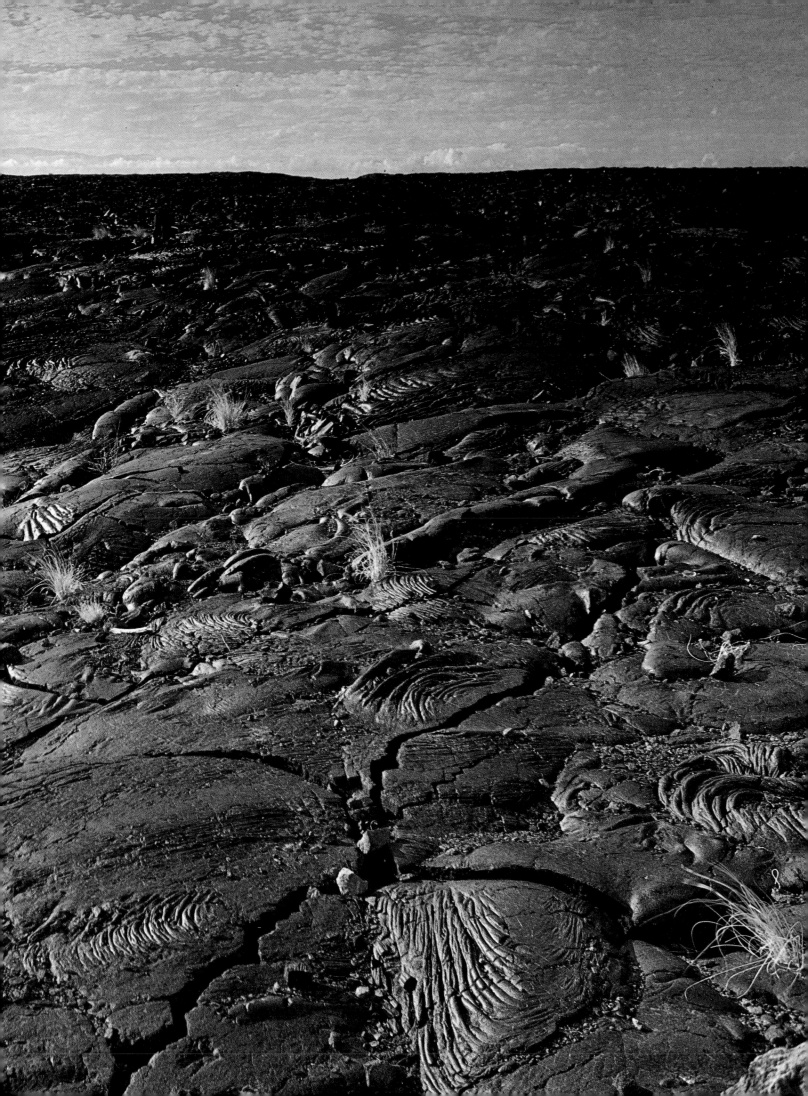

(Previous pages) a vast, solidified lava flow on Hawaii Island. The volcanoes on Hawaii are still decidedly active, spewing lava across the landscape at frequent intervals. Yellowstone is also active: (right) travertine at New Highland Terrace; (below) Midway Geyser Basin; (bottom left) the Opalescent Pool; (far right and bottom right) Grand Prismatic Spring. (Overleaf) Crater Lake, Oregon, the remains of Mount Mazama which exploded with a blast many times more powerful than Mount St. Helens leaving a crater which has since filled with water to a depth of 1,900 feet.

MOUNTAINS

America is a land framed by mountains. Along the western coast stretch the massive Western Cordilleras which reach far inland to the edge of the plains. These are young mountains, having been thrust up only in the last sixty million years, and still bear the scars of their formation. The jagged peaks reach more than 20,000 feet into the air and are riven by deep valleys and sheer clefts. The great forces of erosion have gouged out mighty basins and gorges, but they have hardly touched the heights of the mountains. The formation of these mountains was a long and highly complex series of events which has left massive scars on the face of the west. In parts of the eastern Rockies, vast blocks of rock have been wrenched loose and shoved across the land. The size of these thrust faults is staggering, some being twenty miles wide, 150 miles long and thousands of feet thick. The Cascades are a mainly volcanic range whose mighty extinct and active volcanoes are the result of the grinding together of the American and Pacific plates. Not all the mountains of America are young; inland from the Atlantic coast rise the Appalachians, one of the oldest ranges in the world. The rocks which form the mountains are so old that some predate the emergence of life on Earth. Two hundred and fifty million years ago great forces buckled these ancient rocks and warped them into the distinctive parallel ridges and valleys of the region. The immense period of time which has since passed has worn down these peaks, once much taller than today's Rockies, to the rounded hills of today. Both ranges of mountains have much to offer in the way of scenic grandeur and geological interest and are among the most important of the nation's assets.

(Left) the Watchman, Zion Canyon, Utah.

The great Western Cordilleras (these pages) contain some of the most dramatic scenery in America. In Hidden Valley (center top), Colorado, gentle, forested slopes reach down to Beaver Ponds while elsewhere in the same state the heights of the Sawatch Range tower above the waters (right). Hidden Lake (above) in the mountains of Montana reveals the ancient history of the region. The deep, steep sided valleys, separated by sharp, narrow ridges are typical of once-glaciated areas, while the round head of the valley shows it to have been the start of a mighty glacier.

(Top) Three Sisters Mountain and (left) Mount Hood, both in Oregon. (Above) Medicine Bow Mountains, Wyoming. (Below) the North Cascades Range in Washington. (Right) the Alaska Range. (Overleaf) Mount Whitney, California.

(Left) the Maroon Bells, Colorado. (Center right) mountains at St. Mary Lake, Montana. (Top left) Rockies' foothills, Yellowstone. (Remaining pictures) the Grand Tetons, Wyoming.

In the northern latitudes of Alaska glaciers, such as the Mendenhall (far left), reach down out of the mountains to the sea. Further south the mountain waters are warm enough to form lakes, (above) Sherburne Lake in Montana and (center left) Lake Marie in Wyoming, and to give life to the trees, (left) Yosemite, California. Eventually the waters flow down rivers, (top right) the Rio Grande in Colorado. (Overleaf) Mount Whitney, California.

Wyoming's Grand Teton Mountains are massive blocks of granite which were thrust up from the earth some 65 million years ago, just as the dinosaurs were becoming extinct, and subsequently

eroded into their present peaks and valleys. (Above) the mountains from Oxbow Bend on the Snake River, (top left and center left) from Jackson Lake and (left) foothills in Yellowstone National Park. (Far left) the Lodore Canyon in Colorado. The limestone hills of America conceal a beautiful world beneath the ground. The steady dripping of water through the porous rock has worn away vast caverns, while the deposition of dissolved mineral solids has built up beautiful stalagmites and stalactites. (Overleaf) the Carlsbad Caverns in New Mexico.

The Western Cordilleras stretch right along the Pacific Coast of America. At their northern end the Alaskan mountains, (left) near Valdez, sink into the frozen oceans, (top left) at Norton Sound. In Washington the jagged peaks reach the sky in the North Cascades Range (above), while California can boast of the Chaos Crags (overleaf).

Among the mountains is a
bewildering variety of flora
and fauna. The forest shelters
lupines (above) and the ground
squirrel (facing page, bottom
right), while the streams
offer refuge for the beaver
(facing page, bottom left).
(Top) the Grand Tetons. (Right
and facing page, top) Maroon
Bells above Maroon Lake,
Colorado. (Facing page, bottom
center) the Black Canyon of
the Gunnison, Colorado.

(Top) Sierra Nevada; (above) golden
columbine; (right) Virgin Islands.
(Facing page: top right) Cape
Elizabeth, New England; (top left)
Wooden Shoe, Utah; (bottom) Mineral
Peak, California. (Overleaf) Grand
Tetons, Wyoming.

It is not just the Western states which contain beautiful mountain scenery: stretching through the Eastern states are the scenic Appalachians. This range, far older than the Rockies, contains granite intrusions of immense age. (Facing page, top left) Pinkham Notch in New Hampshire's White Mountains. (Above) Mount Chuksan in the Northern Rockies. (Facing page: center left) Washington Pass, Washington; (bottom left) Kings River, California; (bottom right) Blue Mesa Reservoir, Colorado and (top right) Sarvent Glaciers and Cowlitz Chimneys, Washington.

(Above) horses cross the tumbling waters of Sunrift Gorge in Montana. The Towers of the Virgin (top left) are amongst the most spectacular crags in Zion National Park, southeastern Utah. (Top right) strange rock formations in southern Utah. (Facing page) the rapidly flowing Merced River in Yosemite Valley, California.

WETLANDS

It used to be thought that marshes and bogs were good for nothing except draining. The first settlers to arrive from Europe found thousands of square miles of marsh and swamp on the coastal plain between the sea and the Appalachians. They could not farm the waterlogged soil, nor could they use the timber which grew in the swamps. It was possible to cross the liquid ooze only with great difficulty, and the swamps were breeding places for all kinds of disease. When George Washington came to the Great Dismal Swamp in Virginia all he was concerned with was draining the area for farmland. It is only recently that people have begun to realize the true value of America's swamps. Unproductive they certainly are, compared to rich farming land or oil fields, but they play a vital role in the natural scheme of things. The large bodies of standing water add immeasurably to the water table of surrounding, more fertile land which may dry out without them. Time and again the draining of wetlands has not added greatly to the area of arable land. When the marsh is drained the fine soil is easily eroded and carried away. With the water there also disappears the wetland wildlife, now recognized as one of the richest and most magnificent in America. The massive cypress trees can only survive in swamps, as can a host of other plants. Alligators live all their lives in the wetlands and the birdlife creates a paradise for ornithologists. In Florida, the Everglades sheltered the Seminoles in their long war with the whites and now shelter the alligator and manatee, while the Mississippi brings so much silt and water down from the north that it creates vast swamps and marshes around its mouth which are havens for some of America's rarest animals.

(Left) a section of cypress swamp in the Everglades.

The Mississippi River,
(facing page, bottom left) at
Mayersville, is one of the
great transport routes of
the world. But along its
banks and at its mouth the
great river stagnates into
marshes and cypress swamps
(right). Florida is perhaps
richer than any other state in
wetlands and freshwater
swamps. Cypress trees
(overleaf) stand bedecked with
Spanish moss (below) and great
expanses of water spread
across the landscape (far
right) while birds, such as
the bittern (bottom, far
right) push through the reeds.
The bittern is specially
adapted to life in the marsh.
Its broad feet spread its
weight evenly across the ooze
and the lines on its neck
enable it to merge into the
background by holding its head
up.

The cypress trees, (right) in Desoto Lake, Mississippi, and (bottom center) in Lake Washington, are superbly adapted to life in a marsh. The heavy trees spread their weight across the treacherous mud by means of the fluted and buttressed lower trunks. The larger area of the base makes the tree more stable. The waterlogged soil in which the roots rest is quite incapable of holding oxygen so the cypress roots grow back up above the water surface to form 'knees' (right foreground) which absorb oxygen. (Left) a wading bird and (bottom right) a fish in the Everglades. (Below) a water lily. The alligator (bottom left) is one of the most powerful beasts of the Florida Everglades. It can grow up to 12 feet in length, weigh 550 pounds and is quite capable of attacking large animals such as dogs or even cattle.

DESERTS

The fertile face of America is marred by the existence of extensive deserts, at least that would be the view of any self-respecting farmer. In truth, however, these areas of the continent are among the most fascinating in any land. The well-known Desert of Maine is a misnomer, the area being in truth a stretch of glacial outwash recently laid bare to the elements. The true glory of America's deserts is to be found in the southwestern states where there are thousands of square miles of arid countryside. In such an environment life has difficulty sustaining itself. Plants are few and far between here, with only the best adapted surviving. Cacti have reduced their leaves, through which moisture may be lost, to narrow spikes and are able to store water within their pulpy flesh. Some cacti are pleated so that when it does rain they can greedily suck up the water, expanding to fill the pleats as they do so. More than one traveler has had reason to be grateful for the water-storing capacity of cacti. Animals must be equally well adapted to a dry life. Reptiles and insects thrive in the warm, dry conditions, but even they have difficulty in the burning wastes of Death Valley. These arid conditions favor the creation of strange rock formations. In moister climes the agents of erosion and the proliferation of plantlife would have carved the land in a quite different way. The rough corners would have been worn away and sooth, flowing outlines would have been the result. With just enough water to erode the rocks, but not enough to sustain life, the desert southwest has become a wonderland of nature with carved canyons and monolithic edifices gouged from the rock. The bewildering plant and animal life, together with the scenic grandeur of the areas, have made the deserts of America truly beautiful and awe-inspiring places.

(Left) Death Valley, California, from Zabriskie Point.

(Left) Half Dome, California. (Far left) Superstition Mountains. The deserts of America are a harsh environment for plants, where only specialised species of cactus and water-conserving plants can survive (remaining pictures).

(Right) El Capitan, Texas. (Bottom left) Death Valley, California. (Far right) Blue Mesa, Arizona, where the petrified tree trunks (bottom right) can be found. Minerals have replaced the wood so accurately that individual cells can be made out and studied. (Below) the 'Desert of Maine.'

Water is scarce in deserts, but signs of moisture are all around. The salt deposits in Death Valley (above) are the remains of a dried up lake. After the infrequent rains, short-lived flowers (these pages) spring forth and carpet the desert in color, only to quickly die. (Bottom, far right) Castle Geyser, Wyoming.

RIVERS, LAKES & THE SEA

Water is, perhaps, the single most important influence on the landscapes of America. Without it the continent would be a dry wilderness devoid of life. The forests, swamps and plains would not exist, even the mountains and deserts would take far different forms without the life-giving moisture. Water comes to the land from the skies. Gentle showers may sprinkle water on the land or torrential downpours may batter the soil. Once it has fallen it may be taken up by plants or flow through streams to rivers and lakes. In the mountains the sparkling, tumbling waters gush down the slopes until they splash into the clear blue lakes for which the highlands are so rightly famous. It is the Great Lakes which are the most famous in America for, spreading across more than 94,000 square miles, they have the greatest combined area of any lake system on earth. From the lakes the waters run down to the sea by way of the St. Lawrence. First, however, they throw themselves over a 167-foot precipice to smash down over a 3,600 foot front in one of the most spectacular natural sights in the world: Niagara Falls. Other rivers have equally dramatic courses, flowing through canyons and deserts as does the Colorado. Despite such grandeur it is a slow, sluggish flow which has gained the name "Father of Waters." The Mississippi is so large that it dominates the map of America physically, historically and politically. All these rivers and lakes eventually discharge their waters into the seas and oceans which surround the nation. The coastlines of America include ruggedly beautiful cliffs of stone as well as soft sandy shore and natural harbors turned into ports by man. Water is a ceaselessly active force in America, shaping the land as its flows down rivers, passing through lakes on its way to the sea.

(Left) China Cove,
California.

The streams and lakes with which America is blessed exhibit a wide variety of form. The upland streams of Sol Duc Falls (far left), Washington, and Prairie Creek (top right), California, could easily tumble into a crystal clear mountain lake, such as Bear Lake (left) in Colorado or Mirror Lake (top left) in California. Powerful rivers can carve mighty canyons, such as that (above) in Texas.

The glittering waters in front of Mount Reynolds (top right), Montana, are dwarfed by the Bridalveil Falls of the Merced River at the head of Yosemite Valley, California, (left). Jackson Lake (facing page, top left) and Jenny Lake (facing page, top right) reveal the moods that can come over Wyoming's lakes at different times of day and night. (Above and top left) pebble-strewn Kintla Lake, Montana.

The coasts of America reach across both salt and fresh water: (below) the clear, tropical waters of Leinster Bay and (bottom, center right) Cinnamon Bay, both in the Virgin Islands; (right) the wild and mysterious Pali Coast on the Hawaiian island of Molokai and (bottom, far right) Miners Castle on Michigan's Lake Superior shoreline. (Bottom left) Bear Creek, Colorado.

The jagged peaks and high plateaux of the mighty Western Cordilleras form the watershed for the whole of America. Known as the Continental Divide, this imaginary line marks the division between waters which flow eastwards and those, such as the Snake River, shown (right) in Wyoming near its source amid the Grand Tetons, which run to the west. The Pacific Coast, at which the Snake eventually arrives via the Columbia River, is shown (far right) north of Seattle and (bottom right) at Rialto Beach, Olympic Peninsula, Washington. (Bottom center) Great Bend, also on the Olympic Peninsula. (Overleaf) the serene Beaver Ponds in Hidden Valley, Colorado lie to the east of the Great Divide.

The massive power trapped in
water was once harnessed
at Deadhorse Mill, Colorado,
(bottom right); today such energy
is usually encountered in large-
scale hydro-electric projects. In
many places, however, the waters
are allowed to run free, creating
spectacular results: (left) the
Narada Falls, Washington; (facing
page) the 308-foot-high Lower
Falls of the Yellowstone River,
Wyoming and (overleaf, right) the
Kepler Cascades series of rapids
and falls in Wyoming. (Bottom
left) Crackline Lake in Wyoming.
(Below) Mount Rainier. (Overleaf,
top left) Crater Lake, Oregon has
no inflowing nor outflowing
streams. (Overleaf, bottom left)
snow-laden hills in Vermont.

(Top left) the spectacular peak of Mount Jefferson in the Cascades region of Oregon. El Capitan

(center right), in California's
Yosemite National Park, is the
largest exposed block of granite
in the world. (Center left) a leaf-
strewn stream in Yosemite,
California. (Left) the tranquil
Green River Lakes, Wyoming. (Above)
the roaring Sahalie Falls in the
Pacific Northwest.

Water, whether flowing or frozen, is an important eroding force on the landscape, carving out the valleys and gorges which have added so much to the beauty of the country.

The constant pounding of water
has created some of America's
grandest scenery: (facing page)
Grand Canyon of Yellowstone,
Wyoming; (left) waterfall;
(above) South Fork of Kings
River and (top) Bridalveil
Falls, all in California.

There are many waterfalls in the United States, but the best sited must be the Lower Falls of the Yellowstone (above and right), in Wyoming. Niagara Falls, (far right) Horseshoe Falls and (remaining pictures) American Falls, are perhaps the most spectacular. Dropping 167 feet, the falls have a combined width of 3,600 feet and some of the clearest water in America.

(Above) the sparkling water of Maroon Creek tumbles down the slopes of the Rockies in Colorado.

(Facing page, top) the Upper Yosemite Falls dominate the Lower Falls in California.

(Facing page, bottom) the Continental Divide at spectacular Logan Pass in Montana.

On the Pacific Coast of America lies the ruggedly rocky Monterey Peninsula (above) pounded out of the living rock by aeons of smashing waves. Massachusetts' Cape Cod (bottom center, bottom far right and top right), however, is relatively young. The peninsula is a massive glacial moraine, dating back to the Ice Ages, which rises above the continental shelf to break the surface of the Atlantic ocean. (Right) White River National Forest, Colorado. (Above right and above far right) woodland in New Hampshire's White Mountains.

New England is one of the country's most beautiful areas: (bottom) the strangely colored crumbling cliffs of Martha's Vineyard, off the coast of Cape Cod; (bottom right) a partially dry river in Connecticut; (right) one of Maine's many lakes; (far right) the Flume, a dramatic gorge near Franconia Notch in New Hampshire and (remaining pictures) fall in New England.

Washington is studded with
misty waters, (center left)
Crescent Lake, and Colorado
(far left) with forest-lined

lakes, (left) Granby Lake. Without doubt, however, it is the Mississippi River which is the "Father of Waters."

Rising at Lake Itasca in Minnesota, the river winds 2,348 miles to the Gulf of Mexico and picks up so much

water that it pours 350,000 million gallons a day into the sea. The river has long been an important transport link

and if the romantic paddle wheelers have gone, more freight than ever is being moved by push tugs (above).

(Above) the Gallatin River in Wyoming. (Top right) the Yellowstone River in Hayden Valley, Wyoming. (Top center) Iceberg Lake, Washington. (Top left) Colorado. (Far left, center) the Cascades Range. (Bottom left) Island Lake reflects Sheep and White Horse Mountains in Colorado. (Center left) Kepler Cascades, Wyoming. (Left) Maroon Bells, Colorado. (Overleaf) Kings Creek, California.